WeightWatchers®

Wonderful warming seasonal recipes

Winter Warmers

First published in Great Britain by Simon & Schuster UK Ltd, 2012
A CBS Company

www.simonandschuster.co.uk

Simon & Schuster Australia, Sydney
Simon & Schuster India, New Delhi

Weight Watchers Publications: Cheryl Jackson, Jane Griffiths,
Selena Makepeace, Nina McKerlie and Imogen Prescott.

Recipes written by: Sue Ashworth, Sue Beveridge, Tamsin Burnett-Hall,
Cas Clarke, Siân Davies, Roz Denny, Nicola Graimes, Becky Johnson, Kim Morphew,
Joy Skipper, Penny Stephens and Wendy Veale as well as Weight Watchers Leaders
and Members.

Photography by: Iain Bagwell, Steve Baxter, Steve Lee, Juliet Piddington
and William Shaw.
Project editor: Nicki Lampon.
Design and typesetting: Geoff Fennell.

Colour reproduction by Dot Gradations Ltd, UK
Printed and bound in China.

A CIP catalogue for this book is available from the British Library

ISBN 978-0-85720-932-0

1 2 3 4 5 6 7 8 9 10

Pictured on the title page: Smoky aubergine bruschetta p26.
Pictured on the Introduction: Quick chilli bean filling p42, Baked chicken lentils p64.

WeightWatchers®

Wonderful warming seasonal recipes

Winter Warmers

SIMON &
SCHUSTER
ILLUSTRATED

London · New York · Sydney · Toronto · New Delhi

A CBS COMPANY

Weight Watchers **ProPoints** Weight Loss System is a simple way to lose weight. As part of the Weight Watchers **ProPoints** plan you'll enjoy eating delicious, healthy, filling foods that help to keep you feeling satisfied for longer and in control of your portions.

Ⓥ This symbol denotes a vegetarian recipe and assumes that, where relevant, free range eggs, vegetarian cheese, vegetarian virtually fat free fromage frais, vegetarian low fat crème fraîche and vegetarian low fat yogurts are used. Virtually fat free fromage frais, low fat crème fraîche and low fat yogurts may contain traces of gelatine so they are not always vegetarian. Please check the labels.

※ This symbol denotes a dish that can be frozen. Unless otherwise stated, you can freeze the finished dish for up to 3 months. Defrost thoroughly and reheat until the dish is piping hot throughout.

Recipe notes

Egg size: Medium sized, unless otherwise stated.

Raw eggs: Only the freshest eggs should be used. Pregnant women, the elderly and children should avoid recipes with eggs that are not fully cooked or raw.

All fruits and vegetables: Medium sized, unless otherwise stated.

Stock: Stock cubes are used in recipes, unless otherwise stated. These should be prepared according to packet instructions.

Recipe timings: These are approximate and meant to be guidelines. Please note that the preparation time includes all the steps up to and following the main cooking time(s).

Microwaves: Timings and temperatures are for a standard 800 W microwave. If necessary, adjust your own microwave.

Low fat spread: Where a recipe states to use a low fat spread, a light spread with a fat content of no less than 38% should be used.

Low fat soft cheese: Where low fat soft cheese is specified in a recipe, this refers to soft cheese with a fat content of less than 5%.

Contents

Introduction

Banish the winter blues with *Winter Warmers* – full of fantastic recipes from the best of Weight Watchers cookbooks. From soups to desserts, these seasonally inspired recipes are all easy to prepare and will delight your family and friends.

Winter food can be comforting, tasty and healthy too, and Weight Watchers is here to show you how. Try warming dishes for lunch like the classic soup Bouillabaisse or a Chicken and Bacon Gnocchi Bake. Feed the family with favourites such as Steak and Kidney Pie or Vegetable Masala, or dish up a special meal with Rich Beef and Prune Casserole or Braised Lamb Shanks. And to celebrate, try Roast Turkey with Cranberry Stuffing followed by Christmas Filo Tartlets.

With an emphasis on seasonal ingredients, and plenty of wonderful vegetables, *Winter Warmers* will brighten up any winter's day.

About Weight Watchers

For more than 40 years Weight Watchers has been helping people around the world to lose weight using a long term sustainable approach. Weight Watchers successful weight loss system is based on four tried and trusted principles:

- Eating healthily
- Being more active
- Adjusting behaviour to help weight loss
- Getting support in weekly meetings

Our unique ***ProPoints*** system empowers you to manage your food plan and make wise recipe choices for a healthier, happier you. To find out more about Weight Watchers and the ***ProPoints*** values for these recipes contact Customer Services on 0845 345 1500.

Storing and freezing

Once you have mastered the art of cooking delicious healthy meals, you may want to make extra and store or freeze it for a later date. Store any leftovers in sealed containers in the fridge and use them up within a day or two. Many recipes can be frozen, as can individual ingredients, but it is important to make sure you know how to freeze safely.

- Wrap any food to be frozen in rigid containers or strong freezer bags. This is important to stop foods contaminating each other or getting freezer burn.
- Label the containers or bags with the contents and date – your freezer should have a star marking that tells you how long you can keep different types of frozen food.
- Never freeze warm food – always let it cool completely first.
- Never freeze food that has already been frozen and defrosted.
- Freeze food in portions, then you can take out as little or as much as you need.
- Defrost what you need in the fridge, making sure you put anything that might have juices, such as meat, on a covered plate or in a container.
- Fresh food, such as raw meat or fish, should be wrapped and frozen as soon as possible.
- Most fruit and vegetables can be frozen by open freezing. Lay them out on a tray and freeze until solid, then pack them into bags.
- Some vegetables, such as peas, broccoli and broad beans can be blanched first by cooking for 2 minutes in boiling water. Drain and refresh under cold water then freeze once cold.
- Fresh herbs are great frozen – either seal leaves in bags or, for soft herbs such as basil and parsley, chop finely and add to ice cube trays with water. These are great for dropping into casseroles or soups straight from the freezer.

Some things cannot be frozen. Whole eggs do not freeze well, but yolks and whites can be frozen separately. Vegetables with a high water content, such as salad leaves, celery and cucumber, will not freeze. Fried foods will be soggy if frozen, and sauces such as mayonnaise will separate when thawed and should not be frozen.

Shopping hints and tips

Always buy the best ingredients you can afford. If you are going to cook healthy meals, it is worth investing in some quality ingredients that will really add flavour to your dishes.

When buying meat, choose lean cuts of meat or lean mince, and if you are buying prepacked cooked sliced meat, buy it fresh from the deli counter. Packaged cooked meat usually has salt and preservatives added.

For dressings, choose the best quality balsamic vinegar you can afford and a good quality olive oil. Try a few brands to find the one you like.

Even changing staple foods like pasta and rice can increase flavour. Try imported dried pastas, which have a wheaty bread-like taste and will stay al dente better. Or swap plain white rice for brown basmati rice or jasmine rice and see the difference.

When you're going around the supermarket it's tempting to pick up foods you like and put them in your trolley without thinking about how you will use them. So, a good plan is to decide what dishes you want to cook before you go shopping, check your store cupboard and make a list of what you need. You'll save time by not drifting aimlessly around the supermarket picking up what you fancy.

We've added a checklist on page 10 for some of the store cupboard ingredients used in this book. Just add fresh ingredients in your regular shop and you'll be ready to cook the delicious recipes in *Winter Warmers*.

Store cupboard checklist

- [ ] allspice, ground
- [ ] apricots, ready to eat
- [ ] artificial sweetener
- [ ] baked beans, canned
- [ ] baking powder
- [ ] bay leaves
- [ ] bicarbonate of soda
- [ ] breadcrumbs, natural dried white
- [ ] butter beans, canned
- [ ] chestnuts, canned
- [ ] chick peas, canned
- [ ] chilli powder
- [ ] cinnamon, ground
- [ ] cocoa powder, unsweetened
- [ ] coconut milk, reduced fat
- [ ] cornflour
- [ ] cooking spray, calorie controlled
- [ ] couscous
- [ ] cumin (ground and seeds)
- [ ] curry powder
- [ ] dates, ready to eat
- [ ] digestive biscuits, light
- [ ] fish sauce
- [ ] flour (plain and self raising)
- [ ] fruit, dried mixed
- [ ] ginger (ground and stem ginger)
- [ ] gravy granules
- [ ] herbs, dried (herbes de Provence and mixed)
- [ ] honey, runny
- [ ] horseradish (sauce and relish)
- [ ] jam, reduced sugar
- [ ] kidney beans, canned
- [ ] lentils (dried and canned)
- [ ] marmalade, reduced sugar
- [ ] mayonnaise, low fat
- [ ] mushrooms, dried
- [ ] mustard (Dijon and wholegrain)
- [ ] oil (olive and vegetable)
- [ ] orange segments, canned in natural juice
- [ ] paprika
- [ ] passata
- [ ] pasta, dried
- [ ] peel, dried mixed
- [ ] peppercorns
- [ ] peppers, roasted, in brine
- [ ] prunes (ready to eat and canned in natural juice)
- [ ] raisins
- [ ] redcurrant jelly
- [ ] rice (white and brown basmati)
- [ ] saffron
- [ ] salt
- [ ] sesame seeds
- [ ] soy sauce
- [ ] spice, mixed
- [ ] sponge fingers
- [ ] stock cubes
- [ ] sugar (caster and brown)
- [ ] sultanas
- [ ] sweet chilli sauce
- [ ] sweetcorn, canned
- [ ] tomato purée
- [ ] tomatoes, canned
- [ ] tuna, canned in brine
- [ ] turmeric
- [ ] vanilla essence
- [ ] vinegar (balsamic and white wine)
- [ ] Worcestershire sauce

Soups and starters

Kale and potato soup with salami

Serves 2

157 calories per serving

Takes 20 minutes to prepare,
25–30 minutes to cook

**150 g (5½ oz) potatoes,
peeled and diced**

1 leek, sliced

2 garlic cloves, chopped

**700 ml (1¼ pints) vegetable
stock**

**75 g (2¾ oz) curly kale,
chopped roughly**

**40 g (1½ oz) sliced German
salami, cut into strips**

This interesting combination comes from Eastern Europe.

1 Place the potatoes, leek, garlic and stock in a large lidded saucepan. Bring to the boil, cover, reduce the heat and simmer for 20 minutes. Remove from the heat and roughly mash so that the potato forms a creamy soup.

2 Return the pan to the heat, add the kale and cook for 6–8 minutes until tender.

3 Meanwhile, heat a small non stick frying pan until hot. Add the strips of salami and dry fry until beginning to brown. Serve the soup garnished with the strips of salami.

Tip... Curly kale tends to be a late winter vegetable. If you can't find it, substitute finely sliced cabbage instead.

Bouillabaisse

Serves 2

346 calories per serving

Takes 15 minutes to prepare,
30 minutes to cook

❄ (soup base only)

**calorie controlled cooking
spray**
1 small onion, chopped finely
2 carrots, peeled and diced
50 ml (2 fl oz) Pernod
2 tablespoons tomato purée
**2 garlic cloves, chopped
finely**
**3 beef tomatoes, de-seeded
and chopped**
250 ml (9 fl oz) fish stock
**1 tablespoon finely chopped
fresh dill, plus extra to
garnish**
**300 g (10½ oz) cooked mixed
seafood, defrosted if frozen**
75 g (2¾ oz) frozen peas
1 teaspoon fish sauce
freshly ground black pepper

*The secret to this cheat's version is the splash of fish sauce.
Soak up the lovely juices with a 50 g (1¾ oz) brown roll per
person.*

1 Heat a wide, deep, lidded, non stick saucepan and spray with
the cooking spray. Add the onion and carrots, cover and cook
for 5–8 minutes until beginning to soften. Add the Pernod and
rapidly bubble for 1 minute until reduced.

2 Stir in the tomato purée and garlic. Cook for 1 minute, stirring.
Add the tomatoes and fish stock and bring to the boil. Cover and
gently simmer for 15 minutes until the tomatoes are pulpy.

3 Add the dill and whizz with a hand held blender. Alternatively,
transfer to a blender or food processor and whizz until smooth.

4 Return to the pan and add the seafood and peas. Simmer
gently for 3–4 minutes until the seafood is piping hot and the
peas are cooked. Stir in the fish sauce, check the seasoning and
serve immediately in shallow bowls, scattered with the extra dill.

French onion soup

Serves 4

256 calories per serving

Takes 15 minutes to prepare,
35 minutes to cook

❄ (without croûtons)

calorie controlled cooking spray

600 g (1 lb 5 oz) onions, sliced finely

1 teaspoon caster sugar

1.5 litres (2¾ pints) hot vegetable stock

150 ml (5 fl oz) dry white wine

8 x 2.5 cm (1 inch) slices French stick

50 g (1¾ oz) Emmenthal or mature Cheddar cheese, grated

salt and freshly ground black pepper

Treat yourself to this classic meal of a soup with its strong, satisfying flavour.

1 Heat a large, lidded, non stick saucepan and spray with the cooking spray. Add the onions, sprinkle with the sugar and sauté over a low heat for 20 minutes, scraping the bottom of the pan frequently with a wooden spoon, until the onions are golden and softened.

2 Add the hot stock and wine, season, bring to the boil and simmer, covered, for 15 minutes.

3 Meanwhile, preheat the grill to high and toast the bread on one side only. Place the bread, toasted side down, on a baking tray and cover each slice with the grated cheese. Grill for 2–3 minutes or until the cheese is bubbling and golden.

4 Ladle the soup into warmed serving bowls and float the cheese croûtons on top. Grind black pepper over and serve.

Tip... Onions are an essential store cupboard ingredient and you should always try to keep a stock of them in your kitchen. They are a wonderful base to almost any dish – adding flavour and texture. Experiment to find your favourite – white onions, red onions, shallots, spring onions. Try roasting, sweating, frying – add to casseroles and stir fries or use them to make a delicious soup like in the recipe above.

Spiced beetroot soup

Serves 6
90 calories per serving
Takes 20 minutes

1 onion, chopped

1 parsnip, peeled and chopped

1 carrot, peeled and chopped

2 teaspoons ground cumin

2 tablespoons medium curry powder

1 litre (1¾ pints) hot vegetable stock

300 g can green lentils, drained and rinsed

½ x 250 g packet fresh cooked beetroot in natural juice, drained and chopped

salt and freshly ground black pepper

2 tablespoons finely chopped fresh coriander (optional), to garnish

Finish off this really vibrant soup with 1 tablespoon of 0% fat Greek yogurt and two wholewheat crispbreads per person.

1 Put the onion, parsnip, carrot, cumin and curry powder into a large lidded saucepan. Pour over the stock and bring to the boil. Cover and simmer for 10 minutes until the vegetables are tender. Remove from the heat.

2 Add the lentils and beetroot and carefully whizz in a blender, or use a hand held blender, until smooth. Return the soup to the pan and reheat gently. Season to taste and divide between warmed bowls. Scatter over the coriander, if using, and serve.

Chicken avgolemono

Serves 4
206 calories per serving
Takes 20 minutes

1 litre (1¾ pints) chicken stock
75 g (2¾ oz) dried farfallini pasta
350 g (12 oz) cooked skinless boneless chicken breasts, shredded
3 eggs
juice of a large lemon
salt and freshly ground black pepper
2 tablespoons finely chopped fresh curly parsley, to garnish

This Greek soup is thickened with egg and lemon juice until creamy. Farfallini is a miniature version of farfalle pasta (bows), but you can use any other small pasta shapes instead.

1 Put the stock in a large saucepan and bring to the boil. Add the pasta and chicken and simmer for 4–5 minutes or until the pasta is al dente and the chicken is piping hot. Season generously.

2 Meanwhile, whisk the eggs with the lemon juice in a small bowl. Add one ladleful of the warm stock from the pan and whisk until thinned.

3 Take the soup off the heat and gradually pour in the egg mixture, whisking to amalgamate. It should thicken in the residual heat but, if you need to, place it over a low heat for 3–4 minutes, stirring until the soup thickens. Do not put over a high heat once the egg has been added or it will boil and scramble. Ladle into bowls and sprinkle with the parsley to serve.

Ⓥ **Variation...** For a great courgette and mushroom vegetarian version, see the recipe on page 22.

Vegetable avgolemono

Serves 4
91 calories per serving
Takes 20 minutes
Ⓥ

calorie controlled cooking
  spray
2 courgettes, diced
175 g (6 oz) chestnut
  mushrooms, sliced
1 litre (1¾ pints) vegetable
  stock
75 g (2¾ oz) dried farfallini
  pasta
3 eggs
juice of a large lemon
salt and freshly ground black
  pepper
2 tablespoons finely chopped
  fresh curly parsley, to
  garnish

*This is a fantastic vegetarian version of the recipe on
page 21.*

1 Heat a non stick frying pan and spray with the cooking spray.
Add the courgettes and mushrooms and cook for 5–8 minutes
until softened.

2 Meanwhile, put the stock in a large saucepan and bring to
the boil. Add the pasta and simmer for 4–5 minutes or until it
is al dente. Add the courgettes and mushrooms and season
generously.

3 Whisk the eggs with the lemon juice in a small bowl.
Add one ladleful of the warm stock from the pan and whisk
until thinned.

4 Take the soup off the heat and gradually pour in the egg
mixture, whisking to amalgamate. It should thicken in the
residual heat but, if you need to, place it over a low heat for
3–4 minutes, stirring until the soup thickens. Do not put over
a high heat once the egg has been added or it will boil and
scramble. Ladle into bowls and sprinkle with the parsley to
serve.

Tip... If you can't find farfallini, use any other small pasta
shapes instead.

Stilton and walnut pâté

Serves 2
195 calories per serving
Takes 10 minutes

60 g (2 oz) Stilton cheese
40 g (1½ oz) Quark
1 tablespoon port
1 tablespoon low fat natural
   yogurt
10 g (¼ oz) walnuts, chopped

This is a wonderful treat, especially around Christmas time.

1 Crumble the Stilton cheese into a small bowl. Using a fork, gradually mash the Quark together with the Stilton.

2 Mix in the port and then the yogurt. Reserve about 1 teaspoon of the walnuts and stir the rest into the cheese mixture.

3 Spoon the pâté into a ramekin. Smooth the top and then sprinkle the reserved walnuts over. Refrigerate until ready to serve.

Broccoli soup with cheese clouds

Serves 4

64 calories per serving

Takes 10 minutes to prepare,
  20 minutes to cook

❄

**500 g (1 lb 2 oz) broccoli,
  broken into florets and
  stalk chopped**

100 g (3½ oz) Quark

2 tablespoons skimmed milk

1 garlic clove, crushed

**2 teaspoons chopped fresh
  herbs, plus extra to garnish**

salt and freshly ground
  pepper

This fresh tasting soup is great to fill you up on a cold day.

1 Bring 700 ml (1¼ pints) of water to the boil in a large lidded saucepan and add the broccoli. Bring back to the boil, cover and simmer for 10 minutes. Remove the broccoli from the pan with a slotted spoon and put in a blender, or use a hand held blender, with a little of the cooking water. Reserve the remaining water.

2 Whizz the broccoli for 2–3 minutes, until very smooth and silky. You will need to scrape down the sides of the blender to make sure that all the broccoli is processed. With the blender running, gradually pour in the remaining broccoli water. If you want a really smooth soup, strain the soup back into the saucepan through a sieve – if not, just return it to the pan. Season to taste.

3 To make the cheese clouds, in a large bowl, beat together the Quark with the skimmed milk until you have a soft, dropping consistency. Mix in the garlic and herbs.

4 Reheat the soup gently and pour into warmed bowls. Drop small dollops of the cheese mixture to float on top of the soup and serve at once, sprinkled with the remaining chopped herbs.

Smoky aubergine bruschetta

Serves 2
343 calories per serving
Takes 20 minutes
Ⓥ

275 g (9½ oz) aubergine, trimmed, peeled and cut into thick slices

calorie controlled cooking spray

75 g (2¾ oz) Quark

1 teaspoon smoked paprika

½ teaspoon garlic purée

2 teaspoons tahini

juice of ½ a lemon

2 x 75 g (2¾ oz) ciabatta rolls, each sliced into three across

4 tomatoes, de-seeded and diced

a few fresh basil leaves

salt and freshly ground black pepper

This creamy spread will last in the fridge for 3 days, making it the perfect topping for toasted ciabatta. You could also use it as a dip for four with a warmed medium pitta bread per person, cut into strips.

1 Preheat the grill to hot and put the aubergine slices on a foil lined baking tray. Spray with the cooking spray and cook under the grill for 10 minutes, until cooked, turning halfway through. Remove and chop roughly.

2 Put the Quark, paprika, garlic purée, tahini and lemon juice in a food processor, or use a hand held blender, and whizz until combined. Add the aubergine and whizz again until smooth. Check the seasoning.

3 Toast the ciabatta slices under the grill for 2–3 minutes until golden, turning halfway through. Spread each with some of the aubergine purée and top with the diced tomatoes and basil. Serve immediately.

Variation... Mix 50 g (1¾ oz) diced chorizo with the tomatoes and basil and then use to top the ciabatta.

Brunches and lunches

Potato and chive cakes

Makes 8 cakes
73 calories per serving
Takes 45 minutes

❄

225 g (8 oz) potatoes, peeled
    and diced
100 g (3½ oz) plain flour
½ teaspoon salt
2 tablespoons finely chopped
    fresh chives
1 egg, separated
calorie controlled cooking
    spray
freshly ground black pepper

When you feel like something a little bit more exciting than bread, try one of these tasty little potato cakes. They're at their best served warm.

1 Bring a saucepan of water to the boil, add the potatoes and cook until tender. Drain and mash them thoroughly. Allow to cool for 10 minutes and then beat in the flour, salt, chives, black pepper and egg yolk.

2 In a clean, grease-free bowl, whisk the egg white until it forms soft peaks and then fold it into the potato mixture. Divide the mixture into eight and shape into rough circles.

3 Spray a heavy based non stick frying pan with the cooking spray and heat gently. Cook the potato cakes over a low-medium heat for 5 minutes on each side, until they are golden and cooked through.

Tip... These make an excellent breakfast treat; serve them with grilled mushrooms or grilled tomatoes, or even top with a poached egg.

The big brunch

Serves 1
397 calories per serving
Takes 30 minutes

**150 g (5½ oz) potatoes,
  peeled**
1 teaspoon vegetable oil
½ small onion, sliced thinly
**75 g (2¾ oz) fresh cooked
  beetroot in natural juice,
  drained and chopped into
  small pieces**
**50 g (1¾ oz) thickly sliced
  cooked ham, cut into strips**
**1 tablespoon malt vinegar
  (optional)**
1 egg
**1 tablespoon half fat crème
  fraîche**
**½ teaspoon horseradish
  relish**

*Why not spoil yourself over a leisurely weekend brunch?
It will set you up for the day.*

1 Bring a saucepan of water to the boil, add the potatoes and cook for 8–10 minutes or until just tender. Allow to cool slightly and then slice thickly.

2 Heat the oil in a small frying pan. Add the potatoes and onion and fry over a high heat until browned. Stir in the beetroot and ham and gently heat through for 5 minutes.

3 Bring a small saucepan of water to just below the boil and add the vinegar, if using. Break the egg into a cup and gently slide it into the boiling water. Cook for 2–3 minutes and then carefully lift out using a slotted spoon. Mix together the crème fraîche and horseradish relish.

4 Spoon the potato mixture on to a hot plate. Top with the poached egg and drizzle on the crème fraîche dressing. Serve.

Tip... This makes a tasty supper dish too.

Warm chicken and bacon salad

Serves 1
278 calories per serving
Takes 10 minutes

calorie controlled cooking
  spray
150 g (5½ oz) skinless
boneless chicken breast,
diced
2 x 25 g (1 oz) lean back
bacon rashers, chopped
50 g (1¾ oz) young spinach
leaves or crispy salad
leaves, washed
4 spring onions, chopped
roughly
8 cherry tomatoes, halved
1 tablespoon balsamic
vinegar
salt and freshly ground black
pepper

A fabulous combination of flavours, this warm salad is a
great quick fix.

1 Lightly spray a non stick frying pan with the cooking spray.
Season the chicken and add to the pan with the bacon. Stir fry
for 5 minutes until browned. Meanwhile, place the salad leaves
in a shallow bowl.

2 Add the spring onions and tomatoes to the frying pan and
cook for 2 minutes, stirring occasionally. Add the balsamic
vinegar, bubble for a few seconds and then immediately spoon
over the salad leaves so that they just begin to soften and wilt.
Serve immediately.

Spiced prawn rice salad

Serves 4
388 calories per serving
Takes 30 minutes

200 g (7 oz) dried brown
  basmati rice
25 g packet dried porcini
  mushrooms
150 g (5½ oz) fine green
  beans, trimmed and halved
1 tablespoon Madras curry
  powder
150 g (5½ oz) low fat natural
  yogurt
60 g (2 oz) low fat soft
  cheese with garlic and
  herbs
150 g (5½ oz) frozen soya
  beans, defrosted
100 g (3½ oz) roasted red
  peppers in brine, drained
  and chopped finely
60 g (2 oz) cooked peeled
  prawns, defrosted if frozen
juice of ½ a lemon
salt and freshly ground black
  pepper

This is a great seafood version of the recipe on page 36.

1 Bring a large lidded saucepan of water to the boil and add the rice and mushrooms. Cover and simmer gently for 20 minutes, stirring occasionally with a fork. Add the green beans and simmer for 3 minutes or until the beans and rice are tender.

2 Meanwhile, heat a non stick frying pan and warm the curry powder for about 30 seconds or until the aroma is released. Put in a large bowl and add the yogurt and soft cheese. Stir until smooth and then add the soya beans, peppers and prawns. Set aside.

3 Drain the rice, mushrooms and beans thoroughly and stir into the yogurt mixture. Season generously and stir in the lemon juice. Serve immediately.

Poached haddock brunch

Serves 2
555 calories per serving
Takes 35 minutes

600 ml (20 fl oz) skimmed milk
2 x 175 g (6 oz) un-dyed smoked haddock fillets
280 g (10 oz) spinach leaves, washed
a little grated nutmeg
30 g (1¼ oz) low fat spread
2 tablespoons plain flour
60 g (2 oz) low fat soft cheese
1 teaspoon French or English mustard
1 tablespoon malt vinegar (optional)
2 eggs
salt and freshly ground black pepper

The best dish for brunch. It's filling, but not so heavy that it will send you back to bed.

1 Put the milk and fish in a pan large enough to accommodate the fillets in one layer, skin side up. Bring to the boil, turn off the heat and leave the haddock to poach for 15 minutes. Drain the milk from the fish and reserve.

2 Meanwhile, put the spinach in a large, lidded, non stick saucepan over a gentle heat. Season, add the grated nutmeg, cover and cook for about 5 minutes until wilted. Remove from the heat, still covered, and set aside.

3 Melt the low fat spread in a small non stick saucepan and stir in the flour. Gradually add the reserved milk, stirring well between each addition to make a smooth sauce. Add the soft cheese and mustard, season and stir until smooth again.

4 Bring a small saucepan of water to just below the boil and add the vinegar, if using. One at a time, break an egg into a cup and gently slide each egg into the boiling water. Cook for 2–3 minutes and then carefully lift out using a slotted spoon.

5 Place a small mound of spinach on two plates, top with a piece of fish and then a poached egg and lastly spoon over the cheese sauce. Grind a little black pepper on top and serve.

Tip... Keep the fish warm once you have drained away the milk by covering with foil.

Spiced winter rice salad

Serves 4
328 calories per serving
Takes 30 minutes

200 g (7 oz) dried brown basmati rice

25 g packet dried porcini mushrooms

150 g (5½ oz) fine green beans, trimmed and halved

1 tablespoon Madras curry powder

150 g (5½ oz) low fat natural yogurt

60 g (2 oz) low fat soft cheese with garlic and herbs

150 g (5½ oz) frozen soya beans, defrosted

100 g (3½ oz) roasted red peppers in brine, drained and chopped finely

juice of ½ a lemon

salt and freshly ground black pepper

This warm rice salad makes the perfect light lunch. It will last in the fridge for 3 days and is great boxed up and taken to work to be enjoyed cold.

1 Bring a large lidded saucepan of water to the boil and add the rice and mushrooms. Cover and simmer gently for 20 minutes, stirring occasionally with a fork. Add the green beans and simmer for 3 minutes or until the beans and rice are tender.

2 Meanwhile, heat a non stick frying pan and warm the curry powder for about 30 seconds or until the aroma is released. Put in a large bowl and add the yogurt and soft cheese. Stir until smooth and then add the soya beans and peppers. Set aside.

3 Drain the rice, mushrooms and beans thoroughly and stir into the yogurt mixture. Season generously and stir in the lemon juice. Serve immediately.

Variation... For a great seafood version, see the recipe on page 34.

Warm potato and mackerel salad

Serves 2
531 calories per serving
Takes 25 minutes

Salads served warm or, at the very least, at room temperature, are more flavoursome than when eaten chilled. Try this salad and see.

250 g (9 oz) new potatoes, quartered
200 g (7 oz) green beans, trimmed
½ red onion, sliced into rings
1 celery stick, chopped finely
4 cocktail gherkins in vinegar, drained and halved lengthways
150 g (5½ oz) smoked mackerel fillets, flaked
8 cherry tomatoes, halved
Iceberg lettuce leaves
salt and freshly ground black pepper

For the dressing
150 ml (5 fl oz) 0% fat Greek yogurt
juice of a lime
1 tablespoon chopped fresh parsley
1 tablespoon chopped fresh chives
1 tablespoon chopped fresh mint
½ teaspoon Dijon mustard
2 teaspoons grated horseradish

1 Bring a saucepan of water to the boil, add the potatoes and cook for 10–15 minutes or until tender. Add the green beans 5 minutes before the end.

2 Meanwhile, mix all the dressing ingredients together.

3 Drain the potatoes and beans and toss in the onion, celery and gherkins. Fold the dressing into the potato mixture. Season.

4 Arrange the mackerel and tomatoes on a bed of crisp lettuce leaves. Spoon over the warm potato salad and serve.

Tips... Make sure you don't use creamed horseradish, which has a higher fat content.

Grated horseradish can be found in specialist shops. If you can't find it, try growing your own fresh horseradish. You'll need to peel off the dark skin before grating.

Variation... Replace the mackerel with 185 g (6½ oz) of canned tuna in brine, drained.

Smoky quiche

Serves 8

201 calories per serving

Takes 15 minutes to prepare,
  25–30 minutes to cook

❄

25 g (1 oz) lean back bacon

20 cm (8 inch) cooked
  shortcrust pastry case

1 tablespoon olive oil

110 g (4 oz) onion, chopped
  finely

110 g (4 oz) Quark

60 g (2 oz) smoked cheese,
  grated or chopped finely

2 eggs, beaten

A classic combination, this is ideal for a lunch with family or friends. Serve with a mixed salad.

1 Preheat the oven to Gas Mark 5/190°C/fan oven 170°C and preheat the grill to medium. Grill the bacon for 4–6 minutes until cooked and then set aside to cool. Place the pastry case on a non stick baking tray.

2 Heat the oil in a small, lidded, non stick pan, add the onion and fry for 2 minutes. Cover and leave over a low heat for 5 minutes, until cooked.

3 Meanwhile, chop the bacon into small pieces.

4 In a bowl, mix together the onion, bacon and Quark. Stir in the smoked cheese and eggs.

5 Spoon the egg and cheese mixture into the pastry case and bake for 25–30 minutes or until the mixture is set. Serve hot or leave until cold and then cut into wedges.

Quick chilli bean filling

Serves 1
201 calories per serving
Takes 10 minutes

calorie controlled cooking
  spray
½ small yellow or green
  pepper, de–seeded and
  diced finely
1 garlic clove, crushed
a pinch of chilli powder
½ teaspoon ground cumin
230 g can chopped tomatoes
½ x 410 g can butter beans,
  drained and rinsed

To serve
2 tablespoons low fat plain
  fromage frais
1 tablespoon chopped fresh
  coriander

*If you want to, double up the recipe and save one portion
for another day. Serve with a 225 g (8 oz) potato, baked
in its skin, or with 60 g (2 oz) of dried brown rice, cooked
according to the packet instructions.*

1 Spray a non stick pan with the cooking spray and stir fry
the pepper for 3 minutes until browned.

2 Add the garlic, chilli powder and cumin and cook for
30 seconds before mixing in the tomatoes and butter beans.
Simmer for 5 minutes.

3 Serve immediately, topped with the fromage frais and
coriander.

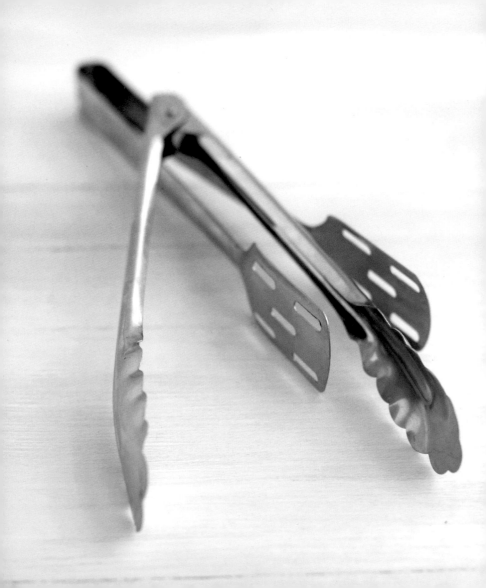

Perfect poultry

Orange mustard chicken with parsnip mash

Serves 1
369 calories per serving
Takes 25 minutes
❄

2 parsnips, peeled and sliced thinly
1 teaspoon wholegrain mustard
2 teaspoons reduced sugar orange marmalade
150 g (5½ oz) skinless boneless chicken breast
1 tablespoon low fat fromage frais
1 teaspoon chopped fresh chives or parsley
salt and freshly ground black pepper

An unusual dish, this sounds fancy but is quick and easy. A perfect 'just for me' supper.

1 Preheat the grill to medium-high. Bring a saucepan of water to the boil, add the parsnips and cook for 15 minutes or until tender.

2 In a small bowl, mix the mustard and marmalade together.

3 Meanwhile, place the chicken, upper side face down, in a foil lined grill tray. Season. Grill for 8–10 minutes and then turn the chicken over and spread on the mustard and marmalade. Cook for a further 8–10 minutes or until the chicken is tender and the glaze has turned a deep golden colour.

4 Drain the cooked parsnips. Mash with the fromage frais and chopped chives or parsley. Slice the chicken and serve piled on top of the mash.

Tip... There is a wonderful selection of mustards to look out for. It's a good idea to keep one or two varieties handy in the store cupboard.

Turkey roulades with mini roasties

Serves 4

452 calories per serving

Takes 15 minutes to prepare,
25 minutes to cook

800 g (1 lb 11 oz) red skinned
potatoes, scrubbed and
diced

1 red onion, half chopped
finely and half chopped
roughly

250 g (9 oz) lean pork mince

1 wholewheat crispbread,
crumbled

½ teaspoon dried sage

calorie controlled cooking
spray

4 x 125 g (4½ oz) turkey
breasts, flattened with a
rolling pin if thick

4 x 17 g (½ oz) slices Parma
ham

4 teaspoons gravy granules

250 ml (9 fl oz) boiling water

freshly ground black pepper

*A midweek version of Sunday roast, without the work. Serve
with steamed Chantenay carrots and broccoli to complete
the meal.*

1 Preheat the oven to Gas Mark 6/200°C/fan oven 180°C.
Bring a saucepan of water to the boil, add the potatoes and
cook for 5 minutes.

2 Meanwhile, to make the stuffing for the roulades, mix the
finely chopped half onion with the pork, crispbread, sage and
freshly ground black pepper.

3 Drain the potatoes, shake to roughen up the edges and then
spread out on a non stick baking tray. Spray lightly with the
cooking spray and roast in the oven for a total of 25 minutes,
adding the roughly chopped half onion to the potatoes after
15 minutes.

4 Meanwhile, spread the stuffing over the turkey breasts.
Roll up and wrap a slice of the Parma ham around each roulade.
Place in a roasting tin, spray with the cooking spray and roast
for 20 minutes below the potatoes.

5 Make up the gravy granules with the boiling water and serve
with the turkey roulades and mini roasties.

Blue cheese chicken

Serves 4

223 calories per serving

Takes 15 minutes to prepare,
25 minutes to cook +
5 minutes standing

❄

4 x 125 g (4½ oz) skinless
boneless chicken breasts

50 g (1¾ oz) blue cheese
(e.g. Stilton), crumbled

2 tablespoons low fat
mayonnaise

4 x 25 g (1 oz) slices wafer
thin ham

1 teaspoon olive oil

salt and freshly ground black
pepper

*Fit for entertaining, these tasty little bundles are perfect
served with a selection of freshly cooked vegetables for a
fantastic feast.*

1 Preheat the oven to Gas Mark 5/190°C/fan oven 170°C.
Line a baking tray with non stick baking parchment.

2 Make slits along the length of each chicken breast to form
deep pockets. Place the blue cheese in a small bowl with the
mayonnaise and seasoning and mix together thoroughly. Spoon
equal amounts of the mixture into each chicken breast pocket.

3 Wrap a slice of wafer thin ham around each chicken breast
and secure it with a cocktail stick. Place the wrapped chicken on
the baking tray and brush with the olive oil. Bake for 25 minutes.
Leave the chicken to stand for 5 minutes before slicing in half
on the diagonal to serve.

Variation... For a tasty accompaniment, mix 4 tablespoons
of reduced sugar blackcurrant jam with 2 tablespoons of
port and 1 teaspoon of finely grated orange zest. Warm
through in a small saucepan and serve a spoonful with
each chicken breast.

Turkey bourguignon

Serves 4

233 calories per serving

Takes 20 minutes to prepare,
2 hours to cook

**calorie controlled cooking
spray**

**4 x 25 g (1 oz) lean back
bacon rashers, cut into
strips**

**225 g (8 oz) button
mushrooms**

2 garlic cloves, crushed

**a small bunch of fresh
thyme, chopped**

**450 g (1 lb) turkey steaks,
diced**

150 ml (5 fl oz) red wine

**425 ml (15 fl oz) chicken
stock**

1 tablespoon cornflour

**salt and freshly ground black
pepper**

**a small bunch of fresh
parsley, chopped, to
garnish (optional)**

*A thick rich stew. Good served with a 225 g (8 oz) potato per
person, baked in its skin.*

1 Preheat the oven to Gas Mark 4/180°C/fan oven 160°C.
Heat a large non stick frying pan and spray with the cooking
spray. Add the bacon, mushrooms, garlic and thyme and cook
gently for 10 minutes.

2 Add the turkey and cook a further 5 minutes. Pour the whole
lot into a deep, lidded, ovenproof casserole dish, season and add
the wine and stock. Cover and bake for 2 hours.

3 Blend the cornflour to a paste with 2 tablespoons of water and
stir into the bourguignon to thicken the sauce. Serve sprinkled
with the parsley, if using.

Variation... For a more traditional beef version, see the recipe
on page 80.

Cranberry duck

Serves 4

496 calories per serving

Takes 20 minutes to prepare,
20 minutes to cook

4 oranges, with finely grated
zest from 2

calorie controlled cooking
spray

4 x 175 g (6 oz) skinless
boneless duck breasts,
trimmed of visible fat

125 g (4½ oz) fresh or frozen
cranberries

500 ml (18 fl oz) chicken
stock

1 kg (2 lb 4 oz) parsnips,
peeled and chopped

300 g (10½ oz) green beans,
trimmed

2 teaspoons artificial
sweetener

salt and freshly ground black
pepper

*Cranberries and orange both work well with duck and help
to cut through the richness of the meat.*

1 Cut away the skin and pith from all the oranges and then
segment, collecting any juice. Set aside.

2 Spray a large, lidded, non stick frying pan with the cooking
spray and heat until hot. Add the duck breasts and sear on both
sides, cooking for 3–4 minutes until brown. Add the orange zest,
segments and juice with the cranberries and chicken stock.
Bring to the boil, cover and simmer for 20 minutes. Remove the
duck breasts from the pan and keep warm.

3 Meanwhile, bring a saucepan of water to the boil, add the
parsnips and cook for 15 minutes until tender. Drain and mash
well, adding a little seasoning to taste.

4 Bring another saucepan of water to the boil, add the beans
and cook for 3–5 minutes until just tender. Drain well.

5 Bring the orange and cranberry sauce to the boil, squashing
the cranberries to release their juices, and simmer for 1 minute
until reduced and slightly thickened. Stir in the sweetener and
taste, adding more if required.

6 Slice the duck and serve with the parsnip mash and green
beans and the sauce drizzled over.

Chicken and mushroom pie

Serves 4
361 calories per serving
Takes 25 minutes to prepare + 30 minutes chilling, 25 minutes to cook
❄

For the pastry
150 g (5½ oz) plain flour
a pinch of salt
65 g (2¼ oz) low fat spread

For the filling
calorie controlled cooking spray
**330 g (11½ oz) skinless boneless chicken
 breasts, diced**
1 onion, sliced thinly
2 garlic cloves, crushed

250 g (9 oz) closed cup mushrooms, quartered
1 heaped tablespoon plain flour
**1 tablespoon chopped fresh sage or
 1 teaspoon dried sage**
**10 g (¼ oz) dried porcini mushrooms, snipped
 into small pieces**
100 ml (3½ fl oz) white wine
300 ml (10 fl oz) chicken stock
1 tablespoon skimmed milk, for brushing
salt and freshly ground black pepper

*Serve this richly flavoured pie with a colourful mixture of carrots, broccoli and cauliflower,
adding 100 g (3½ oz) of cooked potatoes per person.*

1 Sift the flour and salt into a bowl and rub in the low fat spread until the mixture resembles breadcrumbs. Add just enough cold water to bring the dough together. Shape into a disc, wrap in cling film and chill for 30 minutes.

2 Heat a large, lidded, non stick frying pan, spray with the cooking spray and brown the chicken pieces. You may need to do this in batches. Remove the chicken to a plate.

continues overleaf ▶

3 In the same frying pan, soften the onion for 3 minutes before adding the garlic and mushrooms. Cook for a further 2 minutes.

4 Stir in the flour, sage and porcini mushrooms and then gradually blend in the wine and chicken stock. Return the chicken to the pan. Bring to the boil, season, cover and simmer for 15 minutes.

5 Tip the filling into a ceramic ovenproof pie dish with a lip and leave to cool for 10 minutes. Preheat the oven to Gas Mark 5/190°C/fan oven 170°C.

6 Roll out the pastry to a circle slightly larger than the top of the dish. Cut a narrow strip of pastry from around the outside, brush the edge of the dish with water and press the pastry strip on to the lip of the dish. Dampen the pastry border and then lift the pastry lid into place. Press down well and trim the edges. Use a fork to stamp a pattern around the edge and use the pastry trimmings to decorate the top. Brush with the milk and then bake the pie for 25 minutes until crisp and golden.

Chicken, chestnut and winter vegetable stir fry

Serves 4

300 calories per serving

Takes 15 minutes to prepare, 10 minutes to cook

2 teaspoons cornflour

1 tablespoon soy sauce

2 tablespoons sherry or wine

1 tablespoon vegetable oil

350 g (12 oz) skinless boneless chicken breasts, cut into strips

1 garlic clove, crushed

1 red onion, finely sliced

1 large leek, finely sliced

3 celery sticks, finely sliced

1 parsnip, peeled and cut into fine strips

1 large carrot, peeled and cut into fine strips

100 g (3½ oz) red or white cabbage, shredded

240 g can peeled cooked chestnuts

salt and freshly ground black pepper

1 teaspoon sesame seeds (optional), to garnish

Make the most of seasonal vegetables in this tasty stir fry.

1 Blend the cornflour to a paste with the soy sauce and sherry or wine. Set aside.

2 Heat the oil in a wok or large non stick frying pan. Add the chicken and stir fry for about 3–4 minutes, until browned.

3 Add the garlic, onion, leek, celery, parsnip and carrot. Stir fry over a medium-high heat for 3–4 minutes and then add the cabbage and chestnuts. Stir fry for about 3 more minutes.

4 Stir the soy sauce mixture and add to the wok or frying pan. Heat, stirring, until thickened. Season to taste and serve, sprinkled with the sesame seeds, if using.

Variations... Use up leftover cooked turkey or chicken in this recipe – just add it at the same time as the cabbage, making sure that it is thoroughly reheated.

Stock can be used instead of sherry or wine if you prefer.

Chicken masala

Serves 4

349 calories per serving

Takes 15 minutes to prepare,
20–25 minutes to cook

❄ (for up to 1 month)

240 g (8½ oz) dried white rice

1 teaspoon cumin seeds

1 teaspoon mustard seeds

1 onion, grated

2–3 garlic cloves, crushed

2 cm (¾ inch) fresh root ginger, grated

2 teaspoons ground cumin

2 teaspoons turmeric

2 teaspoons curry powder

1 teaspoons paprika

1 small aubergine, diced

2 tablespoons tomato purée

495 g (1 lb 2 oz) skinless boneless chicken breasts, cut into bite size pieces

200 ml (7 fl oz) chicken stock

200 ml (7 fl oz) reduced fat coconut milk

2 tablespoons chopped fresh coriander, to garnish

This is a lovely creamy curry that will happily replace the Friday night takeaway.

1 Bring a saucepan of water to the boil, add the rice and cook according to the packet instructions.

2 Heat a large non stick frying pan and add the cumin seeds and mustard seeds. When the mustard seeds start to pop, add the onion, garlic and ginger. Stir well. Add the remaining spices and stir to mix the flavours together.

3 Add the aubergine, tomato purée and chicken pieces. Stir to coat everything well.

4 Pour over the chicken stock and coconut milk and then bring to a simmer. Continue to simmer for 15–20 minutes, until the chicken is cooked and the sauce thickens.

5 Serve with the rice and the coriander sprinkled over.

◉ **Variation...** For a wonderful meat-free version, see the recipe on page 132.

Turkey chicory bake

Serves 4

309 calories per serving

Takes 15 minutes to prepare,
45 minutes to cook

**calorie controlled cooking
spray**

**1 small red onion, chopped
finely**

**500 g (1 lb 2 oz) lean turkey
mince**

**200 g (7 oz) low fat soft
cheese with garlic and
herbs**

50 ml (2 fl oz) chicken stock

**2 small chicory bulbs, sliced
thickly**

**350 g (12 oz) Charlotte
potatoes, peeled and
cut into thin wedges
lengthways**

*Serve with a generous mixed salad of tomatoes, cucumber,
peppers and herb salad leaves.*

1 Preheat the oven to Gas Mark 6/200°C/fan oven 180°C.
Heat a large non stick frying pan and spray with the cooking
spray. Add the onion and cook for 3 minutes until softened but
not brown.

2 Add the mince and cook for 5 minutes until brown, breaking
it up with a wooden spoon.

3 Remove from the heat and stir in the soft cheese and stock
until smooth. Stir in the chicory and spoon into a 1.2 litre
(2 pint) ovenproof dish. Top with the potato wedges, spray with
the cooking spray and bake in the oven for 45 minutes until
golden and cooked. Serve immediately.

Ⓥ Variation... For a great vegetarian version, see the recipe
on page 138.

Chicken, leek and sweetcorn pancakes

Serves 4
295 calories per serving
Takes 40 minutes
❄ (not filling, see Tip)

100 g (3½ oz) plain flour
1 egg
300 ml (10 fl oz) skimmed milk
a pinch of salt
calorie controlled cooking spray

For the filling
calorie controlled cooking spray
350 g (12 oz) skinless boneless chicken
   breasts, diced
225 g (8 oz) leeks, sliced
1 chicken stock cube
4 tablespoons boiling water
125 g (4½ oz) canned sweetcorn, drained
150 g (5½ oz) low fat plain fromage frais
salt and freshly ground black pepper

This makes a delicious and unusual meal – perfect for a cold winter day.

1 To make the pancakes, sift the flour into a mixing bowl. Make a well in the centre, add the egg, milk and salt and whisk to a smooth batter. Preheat the oven to Gas Mark ½/130°/fan oven 100°C.

2 Spray a non stick crêpe pan or a 20 cm (8 inch) non stick frying pan with the cooking spray. Pour a ladleful of the batter into the pan and swirl to just cover the bottom. Cook for 1 minute and then flip the pancake over and cook the other side for 1 minute. Repeat until you have eight pancakes. Stack them on a plate, cover with foil and keep them warm in the oven while preparing the filling.

3 Heat a large non stick frying pan and spray with the cooking spray. Add the chicken and leeks and stir fry for 5 minutes until the chicken is sealed on all sides. Crumble in the stock cube and add the boiling water. Stir well and cook for about 5 minutes, uncovered, until all the liquid evaporates.

4 Add the sweetcorn and fromage frais, season and warm through gently – don't allow it to boil or it may separate.

5 To serve, remove the foil from the pancakes and divide the filling between them. Fill the pancakes just before you are ready to serve; if you assemble them too early they will become soggy. Roll them up and serve hot.

Tips... To freeze the pancakes, stack them between sheets of greaseproof paper and then wrap them in foil. Place in a freezer bag and freeze for up to 3 months. Defrost at room temperature and then warm through in a frying pan for 1 minute.

If you are unsure about flipping pancakes, do it using a plate. Wearing oven gloves, place a plate over the pan, turn over both the plate and the pan so that the pancake is on the plate, cooked side up, and then slide it back into the pan.

Baked chicken lentils

Serves 4
591 calories per serving
Takes 20 minutes to prepare,
45 minutes to cook

calorie controlled cooking spray
4 x 250 g (9 oz) skinless chicken leg quarters
1 onion, sliced finely
1 garlic clove, crushed
2 x 25 g (1 oz) lean back bacon rashers, chopped
210 g can green lentils in brine, drained and rinsed
200 ml (7 fl oz) chicken stock
1 tablespoon tomato purée
4 tablespoons balsamic vinegar
½ tablespoon dried tarragon
1 tablespoon vegetable gravy granules
4 large vine tomatoes, quartered
freshly ground black pepper

Serve with vegetables, such as spinach, runner beans or carrots.

1 Preheat the oven to Gas Mark 4/180°C/fan oven 160°C. Heat a large, lidded, flameproof and ovenproof, non stick casserole dish and spray with the cooking spray. Add the chicken and cook for 5 minutes or until brown all over. Remove to a plate.

2 Spray the casserole dish again with the cooking spray and cook the onion, garlic and bacon for 4 minutes or until starting to soften. Add a splash of water if they start to stick.

3 Add the lentils, stock, tomato purée, vinegar, tarragon and gravy granules. Cover and bring to the boil. Return the chicken pieces to the top and bake in the oven for 20 minutes.

4 Remove from the oven and scatter over the tomato quarters. Return to the oven for a further 25 minutes until cooked and the sauce is thickened. Adjust the seasoning and serve.

Variation... Use 4 x 165 g (5¾ oz) skinless boneless chicken breasts instead of leg quarters.

Roast turkey with cranberry stuffing

Serves 6

409 calories per serving as suggested

Takes 1¼ hours to prepare, 2 hours to cook + resting

calorie controlled cooking spray
2.5 kg (5 lb 8 oz) turkey, giblets removed
half a lemon

For the stuffing
110 g (4 oz) dried couscous
200 ml (7 fl oz) hot chicken stock
1 onion, diced
75 g (2¾ oz) fresh or frozen cranberries
finely grated zest of a lemon
2 tablespoons chopped mixed fresh herbs
   (e.g. parsley, thyme, sage)
1 egg, beaten

For the roast potatoes
600 g (1 lb 5 oz) potatoes, peeled and
   chopped
2 fresh rosemary sprigs

For the sprouts
500 g (1 lb 2 oz) Brussels sprouts, trimmed
3 x 25 g (1 oz) lean back bacon rashers,
   chopped

To serve
4 heaped teaspoons chicken gravy granules
300 ml (10 fl oz) boiling water

This recipe shows you how to cook a healthier alternative Christmas lunch that is delicious and can be enjoyed by all the family.

1 Preheat the oven to Gas Mark 4/180°C/fan oven 160°C. To make the stuffing, place the couscous in a large bowl and pour over the hot stock. Leave to soak for 10 minutes.

2 Meanwhile, spray a small non stick frying pan with the cooking spray and heat until hot. Add the onion and stir fry over a low heat for 10 minutes until softened, adding a splash of water if it starts to stick. Add the cranberries and cook for 5 minutes or until the skins have burst. Set aside to cool slightly.

continues overleaf ▶

3 Fluff up the couscous and stir in the onion and cranberry mixture with the lemon zest, herbs and egg. The mixture should be slightly sticky.

4 Fill the neck cavity of the turkey with half the stuffing, pulling the skin down and over the bulge. Tuck it in securely underneath. Place the remaining stuffing in a 450 g (1 lb) loaf tin lined with non stick baking parchment and bake with the turkey for the last 30 minutes. Weigh the turkey and place in a roasting tin. Place the half lemon inside the other end of the turkey and spray with the cooking spray. Roast for 2 hours (20 minutes per 500 g plus an extra 20 minutes). Test that the turkey is cooked by sticking a skewer into the thickest part and seeing if the juices run clear.

5 Meanwhile, for the potatoes, bring a saucepan of water to the boil, add the potatoes and simmer for 5 minutes. Drain well. Place in a large roasting tin and spray liberally with the cooking spray. Scatter over the rosemary and roast above the turkey for 45 minutes, turning occasionally until golden.

6 For the sprouts, bring a saucepan of water to the boil, add the sprouts and cook for 3–4 minutes until just tender. Drain. Spray a small non stick frying pan with the cooking spray and heat until hot. Add the bacon pieces and cook for 2 minutes, stirring, before adding the sprouts. Stir fry for 2–3 minutes until beginning to brown. Keep warm.

7 Remove the turkey from the oven and allow to rest for 10 minutes before carving. Make up the gravy with the boiling water according to the packet instructions.

8 To serve, remove the skin from the turkey, carve thinly and serve two 50 g (1¾ oz) slices each with one sixth of the stuffing, potatoes and sprouts and the gravy poured over.

Tip... **Don't forget there are plenty of vegetables you can serve with this meal – try carrots, green beans, cabbage, broccoli and cauliflower.**

Spiced fruity chicken

Serves 4

374 calories per serving

Takes 15 minutes to prepare,
15 minutes to cook

Oranges, apricots, sultanas, spices, chick peas, rice and nuts are all typical ingredients of Moroccan cookery. Try them combined in this easy chicken dish.

2 oranges

100 g (3½ oz) dried long grain rice

2 teaspoons stir fry oil or vegetable oil

350 g (12 oz) skinless boneless chicken breasts, cut into strips

1 onion, sliced

50 g (1¾ oz) ready to eat dried apricots, sliced

25 g (1 oz) sultanas

½ teaspoon ground allspice

½ teaspoon cumin seeds or ground cumin

225 g (8 oz) canned chick peas, drained and rinsed

2 tablespoons chopped fresh coriander, plus sprigs to garnish

salt and freshly ground black pepper

15 g (½ oz) pistachio nuts or flaked almonds, to garnish

1 Finely grate the zest and squeeze the juice from 1 orange. Slice the second orange into eight segments.

2 Bring a saucepan of water to the boil, add the rice and cook according to the packet instructions.

3 Meanwhile, heat the oil in a wok or large non stick frying pan, add the chicken strips and onion and fry briskly for 3–4 minutes, until the chicken is browned. Reduce the heat a little and add the apricots, sultanas, allspice, cumin and orange zest and juice. Cook gently for 5 minutes and then season to taste.

4 Add the chick peas to the rice for the final 2–3 minutes of cooking time to heat them thoroughly. Drain well, add the coriander and stir through.

5 Gently toast the pistachio nuts or flaked almonds in a dry frying pan over a medium heat. Be careful not to let them burn. Set aside.

6 Divide the rice and chick peas between four warm plates. Spoon the chicken mixture on top, sprinkle with the nuts and garnish with the sprigs of fresh coriander. Serve at once, with the segments of orange.

Tip... Don't confuse allspice with ground mixed spice. Allspice is the name of a single spice, sometimes known as pimenta.

Winter chicken casserole

Serves 4
345 calories per serving
Takes 10 minutes to prepare,
   30 minutes to cook
❄

2 teaspoons low fat spread
500 g (1 lb 2 oz) skinless
   boneless chicken thighs,
   trimmed of fat and halved
   lengthways
1 carrot, peeled and sliced
   thinly
1 parsnip, peeled and
   chopped
1 celery stick, sliced thinly
1 leek, sliced thinly
1 large potato, scrubbed and
   chopped
½ teaspoon dried thyme
1 large bay leaf
1 teaspoon wholegrain
   mustard
2 teaspoons plain flour
300 ml (10 fl oz) chicken or
   vegetable stock
salt and freshly ground black
   pepper

This recipe makes for a wonderful and warming family meal.

1 Melt the low fat spread in a large, lidded, flameproof casserole dish and sauté the chicken thigh pieces for about 3 minutes until browned.

2 Stir in the vegetables and 4 tablespoons of water. Cover and simmer for 5 minutes until the vegetables have softened.

3 Mix in the thyme and bay leaf and then add the mustard and flour, stirring well to blend them in. Stir in the stock, season and bring to the boil.

4 Reduce the heat, cover and simmer for 15 minutes until the meat and vegetables are tender. Serve on four warmed plates.

Tip... Mild and wholegrain mustard are great in sauces; they add a subtle bite while Dijon mustards have a lovely, tangy flavour.

Creamy chicken liver pasta

Serves 4

432 calories per serving

Takes 5 minutes to prepare,
15 minutes to cook

350 g (12 oz) dried spaghetti

calorie controlled cooking
spray

1 onion, sliced

300 g (10½ oz) chicken
livers, fresh or frozen and
defrosted, cut into small
slivers

4 bay leaves

1 teaspoon nutmeg

3 tablespoons dry sherry

2 tablespoons tomato purée

2 tablespoons half fat crème
fraîche

salt and freshly ground black
pepper

This is a light version of the classic smooth sauce.

1 Bring a saucepan of water to the boil, add the pasta and cook according to the packet instructions. Drain.

2 Meanwhile, spray a large non stick frying pan with the cooking spray and put over a medium heat. Add the onion and fry until soft – about 4 minutes.

3 Turn the heat down to low, add the chicken livers and bay leaves, season and fry for another 6 minutes.

4 Turn up the heat and add the nutmeg and sherry. Let the alcohol evaporate for 1–2 minutes and then stir in the tomato purée, crème fraîche and 2 tablespoons of water.

5 Remove the bay leaves, check the seasoning, toss the pasta in the sauce and serve.

Marvellous meat

Rich beef and prune casserole

Serves 6

225 calories per serving

Takes 15 minutes to prepare,
1¼ hours to cook

**calorie controlled cooking
  spray**

**500 g (1 lb 2 oz) rump steak,
  cut into 2 cm (¾ inch)
  cubes**

**6 small onions or shallots,
  quartered**

**6 carrots, peeled and sliced
  thickly**

**100 g (3½ oz) prunes in
  natural juice (check that
  there are no stones),
  drained**

400 g can chopped tomatoes

**600 ml (20 fl oz) beef or
  vegetable stock**

grated zest of an orange

**a few fresh thyme sprigs or
  1 teaspoon dried thyme**

1 bay leaf

**salt and freshly ground black
  pepper**

*Serve this rich autumnal casserole with 100 g (3½ oz)
of boiled floury potatoes per person to soak up all the
delicious juices.*

1 Heat a large, lidded, flameproof casserole dish, spray with the
cooking spray and add the meat in three batches. Stir fry each
batch until browned all over and then season and remove to a
plate while you brown the other batches.

2 Return all the meat to the casserole dish and add all the other
ingredients. Stir, scraping up any bits from the bottom of the pan.

3 Bring to the boil, turn down to a low simmer, cover and leave
to cook for 1 hour.

Irish stew

Serves 6

490 calories per serving

Takes 20 minutes to prepare,
1½ hours to cook

❄

calorie controlled cooking
spray

1 tablespoon plain flour

6 x 125 g (4½ oz) lean lamb
chops, trimmed of visible
fat

4 large carrots, peeled and
cut into large chunks

4 onions, quartered

4 celery sticks, cut into 2 cm
(¾ inch) lengths

a few fresh thyme sprigs or
2 teaspoons dried thyme

600 ml (20 fl oz) hot lamb
stock

500 g (1 lb 2 oz) potatoes,
peeled and quartered

2 teaspoons cornflour

1 tablespoon chopped fresh
parsley

1 tablespoon chopped fresh
chives

salt and freshly ground black
pepper

Only a short shopping list is required for this recipe. Choose the freshest ingredients to produce a simply delicious and filling stew.

1 Preheat the oven to Gas Mark 4/180°C/fan oven 160°C. Spray a large flameproof and ovenproof casserole dish with the cooking spray and heat over a moderate heat. Place the flour on a plate and season well. Coat the lamb chops with the flour, add to the casserole and seal both sides, cooking two or three at a time if necessary.

2 Layer all the lamb back in the casserole with the carrots, onions and celery and season. Tuck the sprigs of thyme in between the layers.

3 Pour the hot stock over and then arrange the potatoes on top of the casserole so that they steam while the stew cooks. Bring to the boil on top of the hob and then transfer to the oven and cook for 1¼–1½ hours, or until the meat and vegetables are tender.

4 Carefully pour the cooking liquid into a small saucepan, skimming away any grease, and bring to the boil. Stir in the cornflour and cook for a minute until the stock thickens slightly. Adjust the seasoning, stir in the parsley and chives and pour over the stew. Serve immediately.

Tip... You can purchase fresh chilled lamb stock from most major supermarkets. Fresh stock freezes well, and it is a handy standby at this time of year.

Beef bourguignon

Serves 4

272 calories per serving

Takes 20 minutes to prepare,
2 hours to cook

calorie controlled cooking
spray

4 x 25 g (1 oz) lean back
bacon rashers, cut into
strips

225 g (8 oz) button
mushrooms

2 garlic cloves, crushed

a small bunch of fresh
thyme, chopped

450 g (1 lb) braising beef,
diced

150 ml (5 fl oz) red wine

425 ml (15 fl oz) chicken
stock

1 tablespoon cornflour

salt and freshly ground black
pepper

a small bunch of fresh
parsley, chopped, to
garnish (optional)

*This is a traditional French dish and a variation of the recipe
on page 51.*

1 Preheat the oven to Gas Mark 4/180°C/fan oven 160°C. Heat
a large non stick frying pan and spray with the cooking spray.
Add the bacon, mushrooms, garlic and thyme and cook gently
for 10 minutes.

2 Add the beef and cook a further 5 minutes. Pour the whole lot
into a deep, lidded, ovenproof casserole dish, season and add
the wine and stock. Cover and bake for 2 hours.

3 Blend the cornflour to a paste with 2 tablespoons of water and
stir into the bourguignon to thicken the sauce. Serve sprinkled
with the parsley, if using.

Bacon, mushroom and leek strudel

Serves 4

139 calories per serving

Takes 30 minutes to prepare,
20 minutes to cook

60 g (2 oz) lean back bacon rashers

calorie controlled cooking spray

2 leeks, sliced

500 g (1 lb 2 oz) chestnut mushrooms, 300 g (10½ oz) quartered and the remainder diced

5 x 45 g (1½ oz) filo pastry sheets, measuring 50 x 24 cm (20 x 9½ inches)

2 tablespoons chopped fresh chives

1 small onion, diced

2 tablespoons half fat crème fraîche

1½ teaspoons wholegrain mustard

1 tablespoon chopped fresh parsley

salt and freshly ground black pepper

A scrumptious meaty version of the recipe on page 134.

1 Preheat the oven to Gas Mark 6/200°C/fan oven 180°C and the grill to medium. Grill the bacon for 4–6 minutes until cooked. Set aside to cool and snip the bacon rashers into small pieces.

2 Spray a lidded non stick saucepan with the cooking spray, add the leeks and quartered mushrooms, cover and leave them to sweat for 15 minutes, stirring occasionally. Remove the pan from the heat and leave to cool slightly.

3 Place one sheet of filo pastry on the work surface. Spray it with the cooking spray and then lay another sheet on top and spray again. Repeat this until all the sheets are used.

4 Add the chives and bacon pieces to the leek and mushroom mixture, season and mix well. Spoon the mixture down the centre of the stack of filo pastry sheets. Tuck the sides in and roll the pastry up, completely sealing the mixture in.

5 Place the strudel on a non stick baking tray with the join underneath and spray it with the cooking spray. Cook for 20 minutes or until golden.

6 Meanwhile, spray a small non stick saucepan with the cooking spray and add the onion and diced mushrooms. Stir fry for 5–6 minutes before adding the remaining ingredients. Check the seasoning.

7 When the strudel is cooked, remove from the oven, cut it into four slices and serve each with a spoonful of sauce.

Steak and kidney pie

Serves 6

374 calories per serving

Takes 20 minutes to prepare,
2½ hours to cook

❄

2 teaspoons vegetable oil

700 g (1 lb 9 oz) lean stewing
steak, cubed

2 x 25 g (1 oz) lamb's
kidneys, trimmed and
chopped

1 large onion, chopped

450 ml (16 fl oz) hot beef
stock

2 tablespoons medium sherry

225 g (8 oz) mushrooms,
sliced

1 tablespoon chopped fresh
parsley

2 tablespoons cornflour

225 g (8 oz) frozen puff
pastry sheet, defrosted

1 tablespoon skimmed milk

salt and freshly ground black
pepper

Mushrooms and sherry give a rich flavour to this classic British dish.

1 Heat the oil over a high heat in a large, lidded, non stick saucepan. Add the cubes of stewing steak a handful at a time, turning them so that they seal and brown. Add the kidneys, stir well and reduce the heat a little. Add the onion and cook for another 3–4 minutes or until softened.

2 Add the stock, sherry, mushrooms and parsley to the pan. Bring up to the boil and then reduce the heat. Cover and simmer for 1½ hours or until the meat is very tender. Check the level of liquid from time to time, topping up with a little extra water if necessary.

3 Preheat the oven to Gas Mark 7/220°C/fan oven 200°C. Blend the cornflour to a paste with 3–4 tablespoons of cold water, add to the pan and stir until thickened. Cook for 1 minute, season and then tip the mixture into an oblong ovenproof baking dish.

4 Lay the puff pastry sheet on top of the baking dish, trimming the edges with a sharp knife. Use the trimmings to make leaves for decoration. Position them on top and brush the entire surface with the milk. Bake for 25–30 minutes or until puffed up and golden brown.

Cider pork hotpot

Serves 4
324 calories per serving
Takes 30 minutes

350 g (12 oz) small new
  potatoes, scrubbed and
  quartered
calorie controlled cooking
  spray
450 g (1 lb) extra lean pork
  fillet, trimmed of visible fat
  and diced
1 eating apple, cored and cut
  into wedges
300 g (10½ oz) leeks, sliced
300 ml (10 fl oz) dry cider
150 ml (5 fl oz) boiling water
2 tablespoons cornflour
salt and freshly ground black
  pepper

*Pork and apples are a fabulous combination, enhanced here
by the addition of cider for extra flavour. Serve with steamed
carrots and lightly cooked green cabbage.*

1 Bring a saucepan of water to the boil, add the potatoes and
simmer for 5–6 minutes. Drain.

2 Meanwhile, spray a lidded, flameproof, non stick casserole
dish with the cooking spray, season the pork and brown on all
sides for 3 minutes. Add the apple wedges and fry for a further
minute.

3 Stir in the leeks and potatoes and then pour in the cider and
boiling water. Season well, bring to the boil and simmer, covered,
for 18 minutes.

4 Blend the cornflour with a little cold water, stir it into the
casserole and simmer for 1–2 minutes until thickened.

Tip... For a one pot dish, add the raw potatoes with the leeks.
Cook the hotpot for 5–10 minutes longer, until the potatoes
are tender.

Moussaka

Serves 4

411 calories per serving

Takes 30 minutes to prepare,
45 minutes to cook

❄

**400 g (14 oz) potatoes,
peeled**

1 onion, chopped finely

2 garlic cloves, crushed

**300 g (10½ oz) lean lamb
mince**

**400 g can chopped tomatoes
with herbs**

**150 ml (5 fl oz) lamb or
vegetable stock**

2 tablespoons cornflour

1 large aubergine, sliced

1 egg

**125 g (4½ oz) low fat soft
cheese**

**150 g (5½ oz) 0% fat Greek
yogurt**

**25 g (1 oz) half fat mature
Cheddar cheese, grated**

**salt and freshly ground black
pepper**

*Moussaka is a baked Greek dish of minced lamb layered
with aubergines and potatoes and topped with a creamy
cheese sauce.*

1 Preheat the oven to Gas Mark 5/190°C/fan oven 170°C.
Bring a saucepan of water to the boil, add the potatoes and
cook for 8–10 minutes until just tender. Drain, allow to cool
and then slice thinly.

2 Meanwhile, dry fry the onion, garlic and mince in a large
non stick saucepan for about 5–6 minutes, until browned.

3 Add the tomatoes and stock, bring to the boil, reduce the
heat and simmer for 10 minutes without a lid. Blend the
cornflour to a paste with 5 tablespoons of cold water, add to
the pan and stir until thickened. Season.

4 Spoon half the mince mixture into a large ovenproof baking
dish. Lay the aubergine slices on top. Spread the remaining
mince mixture over them and then arrange the sliced potatoes
on top in an overlapping layer.

5 Beat together the egg, soft cheese, yogurt and seasoning.
Spread this over the potatoes. Sprinkle with the cheese and
then bake for about 45 minutes, until the topping is set and
golden brown.

 Variation... For an equally delicious vegetarian version,
see the recipe on page 137.

Chilli con carne

Serves 4

283 calories per serving

Takes 5 minutes to prepare,
35–40 minutes to cook

❄ (for up to 1 month)

**calorie controlled cooking
spray**

1 onion, chopped

**400 g (14 oz) extra lean beef
mince**

2 teaspoons chilli powder

**1 green pepper, de-seeded
and chopped**

**425 g (15 oz) canned
chopped tomatoes**

1 tablespoon tomato purée

**250 g (9 oz) canned kidney
beans, drained and rinsed**

**salt and freshly ground black
pepper**

*Chilli con carne literally means 'chilli with meat'. This
is a delicious healthier version of this great family favourite.
Serve with 60 g (2 oz) of dried rice per person, cooked
according to the packet instructions.*

1 Spray a large non stick saucepan with the cooking spray and
sauté the onion for 3–4 minutes, until starting to soften, adding
a splash of water if it starts to stick.

2 Add the mince and cook for 4–5 minutes, stirring occasionally,
to brown the meat. Stir in the chilli powder and green pepper.

3 Pour in the tomatoes, fill the empty can with water and add
this to the pan. Stir in the tomato purée and kidney beans,
season and bring to the boil. Simmer for 25–30 minutes, stirring
occasionally.

Tip... Chilli powder is made from dried red chillies and
is used in many spicy dishes. As with chillies in general,
add it according to taste.

Ⓥ Variation... For a vegetarian alternative, use 300 g
(10½ oz) of dried red lentils instead of the meat. Add in
step 3 and cook for a further 10–15 minutes until the lentils
are tender.

Cheese and bacon gnocchi bake

Serves 2

392 calories per serving

Takes 45 minutes to prepare,
20 minutes to cook

**175 g (6 oz) floury potatoes
such as Désirée, peeled and
chopped**

**40 g (1½ oz) self raising
flour, plus 1 tablespoon for
dusting**

1 teaspoon dried thyme

1 garlic clove, crushed

For the sauce

15 g (½ oz) low fat spread

15 g (½ oz) flour

1 teaspoon mustard powder

**300 ml (10 fl oz) skimmed
milk**

**a handful of young spinach
leaves, washed**

**50 g (1¾ oz) reduced fat
Cheddar cheese, grated**

**2 x 25 g (1 oz) unsmoked
back bacon rashers,
chopped into pieces**

*Full of flavour, this is a fantastic dish for a cold winter
evening.*

1 Bring a large lidded saucepan of water to the boil, add the
potatoes, cover and simmer for 10–15 minutes until tender.
Drain and mash. Mix in the flour, thyme and garlic and set aside.

2 Bring another saucepan of water to the boil. Dust a work
surface with the 1 tablespoon of flour and shape the mashed
potatoes into long, thin sausages, about 2.5 cm (1 inch) in
diameter. Cut off 2.5 cm (1 inch) lengths. Resting the gnocchi
on your finger, press the prongs of a fork down on one side.
Add the gnocchi to the boiling water and cook in batches for
2–3 minutes until they rise to the surface. Use a slotted spoon
to remove to an ovenproof dish.

3 Preheat the oven to Gas Mark 5/190°C/fan oven 170°C. Melt
the low fat spread in a small saucepan and then stir in the flour
and mustard powder. Cook gently for a minute and then remove
from the heat. Add the milk a bit at a time, beating the mixture to
a smooth sauce each time. Add the spinach and half the cheese.

4 Spoon the sauce over the gnocchi, sprinkle over the remaining
cheese and scatter over the bacon. Place on a baking tray and
bake for 20 minutes.

Braised lamb shanks

Serves 4

479 calories per serving

Takes 45 minutes to prepare, 2 hours to cook

❄

calorie controlled cooking spray
2 onions, chopped
4 celery sticks, diced finely
2 carrots, peeled and sliced thinly
4 x 200 g (7 oz) lamb shanks, trimmed of visible fat
1 red chilli, de-seeded and chopped finely
8 fresh thyme sprigs, washed and tied together
2 bay leaves
2 garlic cloves, crushed
400 g can chopped tomatoes
300 ml (10 fl oz) lamb or chicken stock
150 g (5½ oz) small chestnut mushrooms
2 tablespoons chopped fresh parsley
salt and freshly ground black pepper

Don't be put off by the long cooking – this delicious and substantial casserole looks after itself for most of that time.

1 Preheat the oven to Gas Mark 4/180°C/fan oven 160°C. Spray a large, lidded, non stick saucepan with the cooking spray and place over a low to medium heat. Add the onions, celery and carrots, cover and 'sweat' the vegetables for 15–20 minutes to soften without browning them. Add a splash of water if they start to stick.

2 Meanwhile, spray a large non stick frying pan with the cooking spray and heat to medium-hot. Season the lamb shanks and brown on all sides in the pan. Transfer to a large ovenproof casserole dish.

3 When the vegetables are softened, stir in the chilli, thyme, bay leaves, garlic, tomatoes and stock. Bring to the boil and then pour over the lamb shanks. Put in the oven and cook for 1 hour.

4 Remove the casserole from the oven and add the whole mushrooms. Return to the oven for another hour or until the meat is very tender and coming off the bone.

5 Use a spoon to skim off any fat from the surface of the sauce and then stir in the parsley. Check the seasoning and serve immediately.

Tips... You can prepare this dish a day in advance up to the point where you add the stock and pour it over the lamb; just store it in the fridge until you're ready to cook.

If you're concerned about the chilli, it adds depth of flavour but not heat.

Boiled bacon with spiced lentils

Serves 4

247 calories per serving

Takes 20 minutes to prepare,
1 hour 20 minutes to cook

❄

**350 g (12 oz) cooked ham
hock**

2 bay leaves

6 peppercorns, crushed

**100 g (3½ oz) dried red
lentils**

1 onion, chopped

**225 g (8 oz) carrots, peeled
and diced**

**1 tablespoon medium curry
powder**

225 g can chopped tomatoes

**600 ml (20 fl oz) boiling
water**

*Ask at your local deli or supermarket deli counter for a ham
hock; they should sell one to you for very little.*

1 Place the ham hock in a large lidded saucepan with the bay
leaves, peppercorns, lentils, onion, carrots, curry powder and
tomatoes. Add the boiling water and bring back to the boil.

2 Cover and cook for about 1 hour 20 minutes, stirring from
time to time. The lentils should be tender and the meat from the
ham should be falling off the bone. Remove the bay leaves.

3 Remove the ham from the pan, shred the meat with two forks
and discard the bone. Return to the pan and stir well. Serve hot.

Cottage pie

Serves 4

475 calories per serving

Takes 30 minutes to prepare,
20 minutes to cook

❄ (before cooking)

1 kg (2 lb 4 oz) potatoes,
peeled and chopped
roughly

1 leek, sliced

500 g (1 lb 2 oz) extra lean
beef mince

1 onion, chopped finely

175 g (6 oz) carrots, peeled
and diced

150 g (5½ oz) mushrooms,
chopped

300 ml (10 fl oz) beef stock

2 tablespoons tomato purée

1 teaspoon Worcestershire
sauce

50 g (1¾ oz) low fat soft
cheese

4 tablespoons skimmed milk

salt and freshly ground black
pepper

A great family favourite.

1 Preheat the oven to Gas Mark 6/200°C/ fan oven 180°C. Bring a large saucepan of water to the boil, add the potatoes and simmer for 15 minutes or until tender. Add the leek for the last 2 minutes of the cooking time.

2 Meanwhile, place a large, lidded, non stick pan over a medium heat, add the beef and onion and brown for 5 minutes, stirring to break up the mince.

3 Mix in the carrots and mushrooms, followed by the stock, tomato purée and Worcestershire sauce. Season, bring to a simmer and cook, covered, for 15 minutes before pouring into an ovenproof dish.

4 Drain the potatoes and leeks and mash with the soft cheese and milk. Season, spoon on top of the mince and spread out evenly.

5 Bake the cottage pie on a baking tray for 20 minutes or until the topping is crisp and golden.

Pork with tomatoes and red wine

Serves 4

210 calories per serving

Takes 10 minutes to prepare,
20 minutes to cook

350 g (12 oz) pork tenderloin,
trimmed of visible fat and
cut into strips

1 large onion, chopped

400 g can chopped tomatoes
with herbs

150 ml (5 fl oz) red wine

1 tablespoon tomato purée

150 ml (5 fl oz) hot vegetable
or chicken stock

1 teaspoon dried herbes de
Provence or Italian herbs

225 g (8 oz) chestnut or open
cup mushrooms, halved

2 courgettes, sliced thickly

1 teaspoon dried sage

2 teaspoons cornflour

salt and freshly ground black
pepper

*Serve with 60 g (2 oz) of dried rice per person, cooked
according to the packet instructions, and fresh steamed
vegetables.*

1 Heat a large, lidded, non stick frying pan, dry fry the pork
and onion for 5 minutes and then stir in the tomatoes, red wine,
tomato purée, stock, herbs, mushrooms, courgettes and sage.
Bring to the boil, cover and simmer for 15 minutes.

2 Blend the cornflour to a paste with 2 tablespoons of cold
water and stir into the pork mixture. Simmer, uncovered, for
1–2 minutes to thicken the sauce. Season to taste and serve.

Tip... Bulk this out for the family with additional chopped
vegetables such as carrots, celery and leeks for a hearty
and filling casserole.

Roast ham with spicy plum glaze

Serves 8
388 calories per serving
Takes 10 minutes to prepare,
  3 hours to cook
❄

**2.25 kg (5 lb) unsmoked
  gammon joint**

For the glaze
125 g (4½ oz) plum jam
2 tablespoons orange juice
1 teaspoon ground ginger
2 teaspoons chilli sauce

Leftover ham can be used for tasty sandwich fillings or tossed into a mid week pasta bake. This makes a great Christmas centrepiece too.

1 Preheat the oven to Gas Mark 5/190°C/fan oven 170°C. Wrap the gammon joint in foil and place in a roasting tin. Roast in the oven for 3 hours (65 minutes per kilo/30 minutes per lb, plus 30 minutes extra).

2 To make the glaze, place all the ingredients in a small non stick saucepan and gently heat together.

3 Remove the foil for the last 30 minutes of cooking, brush half the glaze over the joint and return to the oven, uncovered. Repeat 10 minutes later.

4 At the end of the cooking time, remove the ham to a serving platter and brush any remaining glaze from the roasting pan over the top. Carve into thin slices and serve 175 g (6 oz) of ham per person.

Tip... For a cold eating joint, cook the ham up to 3 days in advance, wrap in foil and refrigerate until required. It is also much easier to carve when completely cold.

Variation... For an alternative glaze, replace the plum jam with orange marmalade, omit the chilli sauce and add a teaspoon of allspice or ground cinnamon with the ginger.

Beef and spinach pasta pie

Serves 4

449 calories per serving

Takes 40 minutes to prepare,
20 minutes to cook

❄ (beef sauce only)

**calorie controlled cooking
spray**

1 onion, chopped finely

**450 g (1 lb) extra lean beef
mince**

2 garlic cloves, crushed

2 tablespoons tomato purée

1 teaspoon hot chilli powder

**4 tomatoes, de-seeded and
chopped**

**3 tablespoons mushroom
ketchup**

**225 g (8 oz) frozen chopped
spinach**

**6 x 20 g (¾ oz) dried lasagne
sheets**

**175 g (6 oz) low fat soft
cheese with garlic and
herbs**

**30 g (1¼ oz) reduced fat
mature Cheddar cheese,
grated**

**salt and freshly ground black
pepper**

*This is a delicious twist on a traditional lasagne. If you
make the meat sauce the day before, the flavours will really
develop. Serve with a garden salad.*

1 Preheat the oven to Gas Mark 5/190°C/fan oven 170°C. Heat
a large, lidded, non stick saucepan and spray with the cooking
spray. Cook the onion for 3–4 minutes until starting to soften.
Add the mince and garlic and cook for 5 minutes, breaking
up the mince with a spoon until browned.

2 Add the tomato purée and chilli powder and cook for
1 minute, stirring. Add the tomatoes, mushroom ketchup and
spinach. Season, cover and cook gently for 15 minutes, stirring
occasionally until the tomatoes have broken down and the
spinach has been well combined.

3 Meanwhile, bring a shallow pan of water to the boil, add the
lasagne sheets and blanch for 6 minutes. Remove the pasta
with tongs and plunge it into cold water. You will need to do this
in batches. Put the blanched lasagne sheets on a board and cut
into 1 cm (½ inch) strips.

4 In a large bowl, mix together the soft cheese, Cheddar cheese
and 2 tablespoons of water. Season, add the lasagne strips and
stir to coat.

5 Spoon the meat mixture into a 2 litre (3½ pint) ovenproof dish
and arrange the creamy lasagne strips on top. Bake in the oven
for 20 minutes until crispy and golden.

Ⓥ **Variation...** You can replace the beef mince with a 350 g
packet of Quorn mince instead and cook as above.

Hungarian goulash

Serves 4
234 calories per serving
Takes 20 minutes to prepare,
  1½ hours to cook
✳

**calorie controlled cooking
  spray**
**400 g (14 oz) lean stewing
  steak, cubed**
1 large onion, sliced
1 garlic clove, crushed
1½ tablespoons paprika
400 g can chopped tomatoes
1 tablespoon tomato purée
**1 large green or red pepper,
  de-seeded and chopped**
**425 ml (15 fl oz) hot beef
  stock**
1 tablespoon cornflour
**salt and freshly ground black
  pepper**

To serve
**4 tablespoons low fat natural
  yogurt**
**a handful of chopped fresh
  parsley**

*Goulash is a rich warming stew that originates from
Hungary. It tastes all the better for its long slow cooking.*

1 Spray a large, lidded, non stick saucepan with the cooking
spray and heat until hot. Add the meat a handful at a time,
making sure that each handful has sealed and browned before
adding the next.

2 Add the onion and garlic and sauté for about 3 minutes, until
softened. Stir in the paprika.

3 Add the tomatoes, tomato purée, green or red pepper and
stock. Bring to the boil, reduce the heat, cover and simmer for
1½ hours, or until the meat is very tender. Check the level of
liquid from time to time, topping up with a little extra water if
necessary.

4 Blend the cornflour to a paste with 3–4 tablespoons of water.
Add to the goulash and stir until the sauce is thickened. Season
and cook for 1–2 minutes.

5 Spoon the goulash on to warmed plates, topping each portion
with 1 tablespoon of yogurt. Serve, sprinkled with the parsley.

Tip... This goulash tastes delicious with 100 g (3½ oz) of
plain boiled potatoes per person.

Beef fillet with horseradish crust

Serves 8
398 calories per serving
Takes 20 minutes to prepare, 1 hour to cook + 10 minutes resting

1 kg (2 lb 4 oz) lean fillet of beef, in one piece
  or boned and rolled sirloin
150 g (5½ oz) mushrooms, chopped
a bunch of fresh rosemary, chopped finely
4 tablespoons horseradish sauce
200 g (7 oz) fresh breadcrumbs
calorie controlled cooking spray
salt and freshly ground black pepper

For the Yorkshire puddings
100 g (3½ oz) plain flour
a pinch of salt
1 egg
300 ml (10 fl oz) skimmed milk

For the gravy
2 teaspoons plain flour
300 ml (10 fl oz) vegetable stock

What's more traditional than roast beef and Yorkshire puddings? A real family treat.

1 Preheat the oven to Gas Mark 7/220°C/fan oven 200°C. With a sharp knife, make a slit along the side of the fillet and then open it up to make a pocket. Mix the mushrooms with half the rosemary, season and stuff inside the fillet.

2 Season the outside of the fillet and then spread all over with the horseradish sauce. Spread the breadcrumbs on a large plate and roll the fillet in them until they are stuck all over.

3 Spray a roasting tin with the cooking spray and place the fillet in it. Cover with a piece of foil.

4 Roast the beef on a lower shelf of the oven for 30 minutes. Take off the foil and brown for a further 15 minutes for a medium cooked fillet. For a well done fillet, brown for 30 minutes. Remove the beef from the oven and place on a carving board, loosely covered with the foil again, to keep warm. Allow to rest for 10 minutes before carving.

continues overleaf ▶

▶ Beef fillet with horseradish crust *continued*

5 Meanwhile, for the Yorkshire puddings, prepare the batter by mixing the flour with the pinch of salt in a large bowl. Make a well in the middle, crack in the egg and then add the milk and 100 ml (3½ fl oz) of water. Gradually stir in the flour until you have a smooth batter.

6 Put a baking tin or patty tin with 12 individual moulds in the oven, on the top shelf, for 5 minutes, until very hot. Using an oven glove, remove the tin from the oven, spray with the cooking spray and quickly pour in the batter. Return it to the top shelf and bake for 40 minutes, until the puddings are risen and golden. Do not open the oven door while they are cooking.

7 To make the gravy, pour off any fat in the roasting tin and then set it on the hob. Sprinkle over the flour and mix it in with the juices using a wooden spatula. Add the remaining rosemary and stock and boil rapidly, scraping up any stuck on juices with the spatula. Season and pour into a serving jug.

Lamb chops with bashed neeps

Serves 4
521 calories per serving
Takes 30 minutes

A deliciously simple recipe that can be on the table in half an hour. 'Neeps' is the Scottish word for turnips. Serve with fresh steamed greens such as broccoli, green beans or spinach.

8 x 60 g (2¼ oz) lamb chops, trimmed of visible fat

calorie controlled cooking spray

2 garlic cloves, crushed

150 ml (5 fl oz) orange juice

4 tablespoons redcurrant jelly

150 ml (5 fl oz) vegetable stock

1 tablespoon cornflour

salt and freshly ground black pepper

For the bashed neeps

450 g (1 lb) turnips, peeled and chopped

450 g (1 lb) carrots, peeled and chopped

150 g (5½ oz) very low fat fromage frais

1 To make the bashed neeps, bring a large saucepan of water to the boil, add the turnips and carrots and cook for 20 minutes or so, until very tender. Drain and, when cooled a little, mash together with the fromage frais and seasoning.

2 Meanwhile, preheat the grill to medium-high. Place the chops on a grill pan and season.

3 Spray a small non stick saucepan with the cooking spray and fry the garlic for a minute or so, until golden. Add the orange juice, redcurrant jelly and stock. Heat, stirring, until the jelly has dissolved. Mix the cornflour with 2 tablespoons of cold water to make a paste and then add to the other ingredients in the pan. Bring the sauce to the boil, stirring until it thickens. Season.

4 Meanwhile, grill the chops for 3–4 minutes on each side until golden, seasoning when you turn them.

5 Serve the chops with the bashed neeps and sauce.

Sausages with roasted vegetable Yorkshires

Serves 4

393 calories per serving

Takes 50 minutes

4 carrots, peeled and chopped into 2 cm (¾ inch) chunks

4 parsnips (180 g/6 oz), peeled and chopped into 2 cm (¾ inch) chunks

450 g (1 lb) butternut squash, peeled, de-seeded and chopped into 2 cm (¾ inch) chunks

calorie controlled cooking spray

60 g (2 oz) plain flour

1 egg

150 ml (5 fl oz) skimmed milk

1 onion, chopped roughly

8 thick low fat pork sausages such as Weight Watchers Premium Pork Sausages

4 teaspoons gravy granules

250 ml (9 fl oz) boiling water

salt and freshly ground black pepper

This recipe is particularly good served with a heap of lightly steamed green cabbage.

1 Preheat the oven to Gas Mark 7/220°C/fan oven 200°C. Spread the carrots, parsnips and squash out on a baking tray, season with black pepper and spray lightly with the cooking spray. Roast in the oven for 15 minutes on the middle shelf.

2 To make the Yorkshire pudding batter, sift the flour into a mixing bowl and make a well in the centre. Add the egg and gradually mix in the milk to give a smooth batter. Season and set aside.

3 When the 15 minutes are up, stir the onion in with the other vegetables and add the sausages to the tray. Return to the oven and cook for 5 minutes. At the same time, pop a 20 cm (8 inch) square tin or a four hole Yorkshire pudding tin on the top shelf to preheat.

4 When the tin is hot, quickly spray with the cooking spray, pour in the batter and return to the oven. Cook above the tray of sausages and vegetables for 15 minutes until risen and crisp and the sausages are cooked.

5 Meanwhile, make up the gravy granules with the boiling water according to the packet instructions.

6 Divide the Yorkshire pudding into four (or serve one Yorkshire pudding each) and pile the roasted vegetables on top. Serve each one with two sausages, with the gravy poured over.

Beef in beer with mustard and thyme dumplings

Serves 4

354 calories per serving

Takes 25 minutes to prepare, 1 hour 45 minutes to cook

❄ (beef in beer only)

400 g (14 oz) lean casserole steak, cubed
calorie controlled cooking spray
1 onion, cut into wedges
2 celery sticks, chopped
2 leeks, cut into chunks
3 carrots, peeled and cut into chunks
1 heaped tablespoon plain flour
300 ml (10 fl oz) beer or ale
600 ml (20 fl oz) beef stock
175 g (6 oz) mushrooms, sliced thickly
salt and freshly ground black pepper

For the dumplings
110 g (4 oz) self raising flour
½ teaspoon baking powder
a pinch of salt
½ tablespoon chopped fresh thyme leaves
1 tablespoon wholegrain mustard
50 g (1¾ oz) low fat spread

Melt in the mouth dumplings top this hearty casserole – all you need to go with it is a big bowl of green cabbage.

1 Heat a non stick frying pan and dry fry the meat in batches, removing the meat to a plate when it is well browned all over. Preheat the oven to Gas Mark 2/150°C/fan oven 130°C.

2 Heat an lidded flameproof and ovenproof casserole dish, spray with the cooking spray, add the onion wedges and brown well on both sides.

3 Heat a large non stick saucepan and spray with the cooking spray. Add the celery, leeks and carrots and cook for 2 minutes until lightly browned. Stir in the flour and then gradually blend in the beer or ale and stock. Pour everything into the casserole dish and then add the browned meat. Season, stir well and bring the sauce to a simmer. Cover the casserole and transfer to the oven to cook for 1 hour 15 minutes.

4 To make the dumplings, sift the flour, baking powder and the pinch of salt into a mixing bowl. Stir in the thyme and mustard and then rub in the low fat spread until the mixture resembles breadcrumbs. Add just enough cold water to bring the mixture together as a soft dough and shape into eight dumplings.

5 Remove the casserole from the oven, stir the mushrooms into the sauce and arrange the dumplings on top. Replace the lid, return to the oven and cook for 30 minutes.

Fish and seafood

Colcannon with prawns

Serves 1

339 calories per serving

Takes 30 minutes

200 g (7 oz) potatoes, peeled and cubed

a few leaves of Savoy or other cabbage, shredded

75 ml (3 fl oz) skimmed milk

1 small leek, chopped

calorie controlled cooking spray

1 garlic clove, chopped

100 g (3½ oz) raw peeled prawns, defrosted if frozen

juice of ½ a lemon

1 teaspoon French mustard

salt and freshly ground black pepper

Colcannon is a hearty Irish potato dish with cabbage and leeks. Here we add prawns to make a very satisfying supper.

1 Bring two saucepans of water to the boil, add the potatoes and cabbage, separately, and cook for about 15 minutes each, or until soft. Drain.

2 Meanwhile, in a small lidded saucepan, heat the milk with the leek for 5 minutes, covered, until the leek is softened.

3 Spray a non stick frying pan with the cooking spray and fry the garlic until golden. Add the prawns and stir fry for 2–3 minutes or until pink and cooked through. Pour over the lemon juice and season.

4 Mash the potatoes with the leek and milk and then stir in the drained cabbage and mustard and season. Spoon on to a plate and make a little well in the centre. Fill with the prawns and their juices and serve.

Oven baked fish and chips

Serves 4
373 calories per serving
Takes 10 minutes to prepare,
45 minutes to cook

500 g (1 lb 2 oz) potatoes,
  peeled and cut into 1 cm
  (¼ inch) thick chips
calorie controlled cooking
  spray
4 x 150 g (5½ oz) skinless
  cod loin fillets
50 g (1¾ oz) low fat spread
100 g (3½ oz) plain flour
½ teaspoon bicarbonate of
  soda
1 egg, beaten
50 ml (2 fl oz) beer
salt and freshly ground black
  pepper
lemon wedges, to serve

Enjoy delicious, home made, golden and crispy beer batter, without a deep fat fryer in sight. For the full experience, serve with 70 g (2½ oz) of cooked peas per person, using a food processor, or a hand held blender, until mushy, along with grilled tomato halves.

1 Preheat the oven to Gas Mark 7/220°C/fan oven 200°C. Arrange the chips in a single layer on a non stick baking tray. Spray with the cooking spray and bake in the oven for 25–30 minutes, turning halfway, until golden and crispy.

2 Meanwhile, arrange the cod fillets on another non stick baking tray. In a bowl, cream together the low fat spread, flour and bicarbonate of soda. Beat in the egg until smooth and then mix in the beer until you get a thick batter.

3 After 30 minutes, put the chips on the lowest shelf in the oven. Spread the batter in a thick layer over the top of each cod fillet, trying not to let it go on the tray. Bake in the oven on a high shelf for 10–15 minutes, until puffed up and golden. Serve immediately with the chips and lemon wedges on the side.

Smoked fish pie

Serves 6

367 calories per serving

Takes 30 minutes to prepare, 25 minutes to cook

❄ (before cooking)

600 g (1 lb 5 oz) smoked haddock fillets
500 ml (18 fl oz) skimmed milk
1.25 kg (2 lb 12 oz) floury potatoes
(e.g. Desirée or Maris Piper), peeled
and cut into chunks
2 tablespoons chopped fresh chives
1 tablespoon wholegrain mustard (optional)
2 teaspoons low fat spread
3 leeks, sliced

100 g (3½ oz) smoked salmon, chopped
roughly
2 tablespoons cornflour
½ fish stock cube
juice of ½ a lemon
50 g (1¾ oz) low fat soft cheese
freshly ground black pepper

A fantastic family favourite, this smoked fish pie is impressive enough to serve up when you are entertaining. Serve with a variety of vegetables.

1 Preheat the oven to Gas Mark 4/180°C/fan oven 160°C. Place the smoked haddock in a roasting tin and season with black pepper.

2 Reserve 4 tablespoons of milk for the potato topping and pour the remainder over the fish. Bake for 12 minutes or until the fish flakes easily. Using a fish slice, carefully lift the fish on to a plate to cool slightly and strain the milk into a jug.

3 Meanwhile, bring a large saucepan of water to the boil, add the potatoes and cook for 15–20 minutes or until tender. Drain and mash with the reserved milk. Mix in the chives and mustard, if using.

continues overleaf ▶

4 While the potatoes are cooking, melt the low fat spread in a lidded non stick saucepan and stir in the leeks. Season with black pepper and add 2 tablespoons of water. Cover and cook gently for 5 minutes.

5 Using two forks, pull the smoked haddock away from its skin and break into large flakes. Place in an ovenproof baking dish, add the smoked salmon and leeks and mix together.

6 In a small bowl, blend the cornflour with a little of the strained milk, add back into the rest of the milk and pour into the pan that the leeks were cooked in. Crumble in the fish stock cube and bring the sauce to a simmer, stirring until thickened. Simmer for 3 minutes and then whisk in the lemon juice and soft cheese until smooth. Pour this over the fish mixture and spread the mashed potatoes on top.

7 Put the dish on a baking tray in the oven and cook for 25 minutes until golden.

Tip... Smoked salmon trimmings are a good option in this recipe and will cost a lot less than the sliced version.

Cod and parsley fish cakes

Serves 4
268 calories per serving
Takes 40 minutes to prepare,
20 minutes to cook
❄

450 g (1 lb) potatoes, peeled
and diced
300 g (10½ oz) skinless cod
fillet
3 lemon slices
2 tablespoons chopped fresh
parsley
1 teaspoon horseradish
sauce
1 egg, beaten
75 g (2¾ oz) natural dried
white breadcrumbs
2 tablespoons plain flour
calorie controlled cooking
spray
salt and freshly ground black
pepper

These delicious home made fish cakes, served warm with a crisp green salad garnish, make a filling lunch or light supper.

1 Bring a saucepan of water to the boil, add the potatoes and cook for 12–15 minutes until tender. Drain and mash thoroughly.

2 Place the cod with the lemon slices in a large frying pan and cover with water. Bring to the boil and then reduce the heat and simmer for 5 minutes, until the fish is cooked. Drain well, discarding the lemon, and flake the fish. Preheat the oven to Gas Mark 5/190°C/fan oven 170°C.

3 Add the fish, parsley, horseradish sauce and seasoning to the mashed potatoes and mix together thoroughly. Divide the mixture into eight and then shape into small, round, flat cakes with your hands. Line a baking tray with non stick baking parchment. Place the beaten egg in a shallow bowl and the breadcrumbs in another.

4 Dust the fish cakes with the flour and then dip them in the beaten egg followed by the breadcrumbs. Place them on the baking tray and spray with the cooking spray.

5 Bake the fish cakes in the oven for 20 minutes, turning halfway through and spraying again with the cooking spray if necessary, until the breadcrumbs have turned golden and crisp.

Tip... You can buy natural dried breadcrumbs in supermarkets. They have a better flavour than the bright yellow variety.

Roast trout with orange and ginger sauce

Serves 2
305 calories per serving
Takes 15 minutes

calorie controlled cooking
  spray
2 x 150 g (5½ oz) pink trout
  fillets
200 g (7 oz) fine green beans,
  trimmed
salt and freshly ground black
  pepper
1 teaspoon sesame seeds, to
  garnish

For the orange and ginger
sauce
juice of ¼ of a lemon
2 tablespoons fresh orange
  juice
1 teaspoon honey
½ teaspoon sesame oil
1 tablespoon soy sauce
2.5 cm (1 inch) fresh root
  ginger, cut into matchsticks

*Serve with 60 g (2 oz) of dried egg noodles per person,
cooked according to the packet instructions.*

1 Preheat the oven to Gas Mark 6/200°C/fan oven 180°C.
Spray a roasting tin with the cooking spray. Put the trout fillets
in the tin, skin side down, season and spray with the cooking
spray. Roast for 10–12 minutes, depending on the thickness
of the fillets.

2 Meanwhile, bring a saucepan of water to the boil, add the
green beans and cook for 4–5 minutes or until tender. Drain.

3 To make the orange and ginger sauce, put all the ingredients
in a small non stick saucepan and bring up to the boil. Reduce
the heat and simmer, stirring occasionally, for about 3 minutes
until reduced and slightly thickened.

4 Place the green beans on serving plates, top with the trout
fillets and spoon over the sauce. Sprinkle with the sesame
seeds before serving.

Moules Provençales

Serves 4

96 calories per serving

Takes 10 minutes to prepare,
15 minutes to cook

calorie controlled cooking
spray

2 garlic cloves, chopped
finely

1 onion, chopped finely

150 ml (5 fl oz) fish or
vegetable stock

400 g can chopped tomatoes

a bunch of fresh basil or
thyme, chopped

1 kg (2 lb 4 oz) mussels,
washed (see Tip)

salt and freshly ground black
pepper

*Serve with a 50 g (1¾ oz) crusty roll per person to mop up
the juice.*

1 Spray a large, lidded, non stick saucepan with the cooking
spray and sauté the garlic and onion for 5 minutes until soft,
adding a splash of water if they start to stick.

2 Add the stock, tomatoes and herbs, season and cook briskly
for 5 minutes. Add the mussels, cover and continue to cook for
another 5 minutes, shaking the pan vigorously a few times.

3 When you remove the lid, the mussels should have opened.
Any that have not opened should be discarded. Spoon into
serving bowls.

Tip... To prepare mussels, scrub off any dirt and remove any
barnacles. Remove the beard, if any, that sticks out between
the shells. Discard any mussels that are already open or
have a cracked shell.

Variation... Replace the stock with white wine.

Winter seafood stew

Serves 4
248 calories per serving
Takes 25 minutes

1 tablespoon olive oil
2 shallots or 1 onion, chopped finely
425 ml (15 fl oz) good quality fish or vegetable stock
4 tablespoons white wine
a large pinch of saffron strands (optional)
grated zest of ½ a lemon
225 g (8 oz) salmon fillets, skinned and cut into 4 cm (1½ inch) chunks
225 g (8 oz) cod fillets, skinned and cut into 4 cm (1½ inch) chunks
2 tablespoons half fat crème fraîche
100 g (3½ oz) cooked peeled prawns, defrosted if frozen
salt and freshly ground black pepper
1 tablespoon chopped fresh parsley or dill, to garnish

This is a delicious 'stew' – good enough to serve on special occasions. As with all fish recipes, your choice of fish can be flexible to suit availability and preference. Try adding fresh mussels, which are in season over the winter months.

1 Heat the oil in a large, lidded, non stick pan and gently cook the shallots or onion for 4–5 minutes until softened but not coloured. Add a splash of water if they start to stick.

2 Add the stock, wine, saffron (if using) and lemon zest and season lightly. Bring to a gentle simmer and add the salmon and cod. Cover and poach for 2–3 minutes or until the fish becomes opaque. Using a slotted spoon, carefully remove the fish and keep warm.

3 Boil the stock rapidly to reduce it to approximately 300 ml (10 fl oz). Reduce the heat, stir in the crème fraîche and return the fish, together with the prawns, to the pan. Heat through for 3–4 minutes. Adjust the seasoning to taste and serve, garnished with the parsley or dill.

Tuna pasta bake

Serves 2
362 calories per serving
Takes 20 minutes to prepare,
35–40 minutes to cook
❄

100 g (3½ oz) dried pasta
  shapes
100 g (3½ oz) broccoli, cut
  into florets
calorie controlled cooking
  spray
200 g can tuna in brine,
  drained
1 large egg
150 ml (5 fl oz) skimmed
  milk
1 tablespoon chopped fresh
  parsley
25 g (1 oz) half fat mature
  Cheddar cheese, grated
salt and freshly ground black
  pepper

A twist on the old tuna and sweetcorn favourite.

1 Preheat the oven to Gas Mark 5/190°C/fan oven 170°C.

2 Bring a saucepan of water to the boil, add the pasta and cook according to the packet instructions. Drain well.

3 Meanwhile, bring another saucepan of water to the boil, add the broccoli and cook for about 6 minutes. Drain well.

4 Spray a 600ml (20 fl oz) ovenproof dish with the cooking spray. Flake the tuna into the dish and mix in the pasta and broccoli.

5 Beat the egg with the milk and parsley and season. Pour into the dish and sprinkle the cheese over the top. Bake for 35–40 minutes, until set and golden.

Simply vegetarian

Leek and butter bean crumble

Serves 2
222 calories per serving
Takes 25 minutes

calorie controlled cooking spray
250 g (9 oz) leeks, sliced
150 ml (5 fl oz) vegetable stock
1 medium slice wholemeal bread, torn into pieces
40 g (1½ oz) half fat mature Cheddar cheese, grated
410 g can butter beans, drained and rinsed
2 teaspoons wholegrain mustard
salt and freshly ground black pepper

This rustic dish with a cheesy crust is perfect served with steamed broccoli florets.

1 Preheat the oven to Gas Mark 5/190°C/fan oven 170°C. Lightly spray a lidded non stick saucepan with the cooking spray, add the leeks, season and toss to coat. Add 3 tablespoons of the stock, cover the pan and cook for 4 minutes until tender.

2 Meanwhile, whizz the bread to crumbs in a food processor, or use a hand held blender. Mix with the grated cheese.

3 Add the butter beans, mustard and remaining stock to the leeks, season and stir to mix. Tip into an ovenproof baking dish. Cover with the cheesy crumbs and spray with the cooking spray. Bake for 15 minutes until crisp, golden and bubbling.

Winter vegetable pasta

Serves 4
526 calories per serving
Takes 45–60 minutes

Winter vegetables are cooked until meltingly soft and then tossed with low fat soft cheese to make a comforting warming pasta for winter nights.

1 Preheat the oven to Gas Mark 6/200°C/fan oven 180°C. Put the vegetables and garlic in a large non stick roasting tin, season, sprinkle over the rosemary and spray with the cooking spray. Roast in the oven for 45–60 minutes or until the vegetables are soft.

2 About 10–15 minutes before the end of the roasting time, bring a saucepan of water to the boil, add the pasta and cook according to the packet instructions. Drain.

3 Toss the pasta with the vegetables in the roasting tin and stir in the soft cheese. Check the seasoning and serve.

6 carrots, peeled and cut into quarters or sixths lengthways

4 parsnips, peeled and cut into quarters or sixths lengthways

2 onions, cut into eighths

1 small pumpkin or squash, peeled, de-seeded and cut into bite size pieces

450 g (1 lb) Brussels sprouts, halved

8 garlic cloves, smashed

leaves from 4 fresh rosemary sprigs or 2 teaspoons dried rosemary

calorie controlled cooking spray

350 g (12 oz) dried pasta

100 g (3½ oz) low fat soft cheese

salt and freshly ground black pepper

Vegetable masala

Serves 4

406 calories per serving

Takes 15 minutes to prepare,
15–20 minutes to cook

❄ (for up to 1 month)

240 g (8½ oz) dried white rice
1 teaspoon cumin seeds
1 teaspoon mustard seeds
1 onion, grated
2–3 garlic cloves, crushed
2 cm (¾ inch) fresh root
    ginger, grated
2 teaspoons ground cumin
2 teaspoons turmeric
2 teaspoons curry powder
1 teaspoons paprika
1 small aubergine, diced
2 tablespoons tomato purée
1 kg (2 lb 4 oz) potatoes,
    peeled and cut into bite
    size pieces
200 ml (7 fl oz) vegetable
    stock
200 ml (7 fl oz) reduced fat
    coconut milk
2 tablespoons chopped fresh
    coriander, to garnish

Tasty and filling, this is a vegetarian version of the recipe on page 58.

1 Bring a saucepan of water to the boil, add the rice and cook according to the packet instructions.

2 Heat a large non stick frying pan and add the cumin seeds and mustard seeds. When the mustard seeds start to pop, add the onion, garlic and ginger. Stir well. Add the remaining spices and stir to mix the flavours together.

3 Add the aubergine, tomato purée and potatoes. Stir to coat everything well.

4 Pour over the vegetable stock and coconut milk and then bring to a simmer. Continue to simmer for 10–15 minutes, until the potatoes are cooked and the sauce thickens.

5 Serve with the rice and the coriander sprinkled over.

Rich mushroom and prune casserole

Serves 6

90 calories per serving

Takes 15 minutes to prepare,
45 minutes to cook

❄

calorie controlled cooking
spray

450 g (1 lb) mushrooms,
halved or quartered if large

6 small onions or shallots,
quartered

6 carrots, peeled and sliced
thickly

100 g (3½ oz) prunes in
natural juice (check that
there are no stones),
drained

400 g can chopped tomatoes

600 ml (20 fl oz) vegetable
stock

grated zest of an orange

a few fresh thyme sprigs or
1 teaspoon dried thyme

1 bay leaf

salt and freshly ground black
pepper

Serve this vegetarian version of the Rich beef and prune casserole on page 76 with 100 g (3½ oz) of boiled floury potatoes per person to soak up all the delicious juices.

1 Heat a large, lidded, flameproof casserole dish, spray with the cooking spray and add the mushrooms in three batches. Stir fry each batch until softened and then season and remove to a plate while you brown the other batches.

2 Return all the mushrooms to the casserole dish and add all the other ingredients. Stir, scraping up any bits from the bottom of the pan.

3 Bring to the boil, turn down to a low simmer, cover and leave to cook for 30 minutes.

Stilton, mushroom and leek strudel

Serves 4

188 calories per serving

Takes 30 minutes to prepare,
   20 minutes to cook

calorie controlled cooking
   spray

2 leeks, sliced

500 g (1 lb 2 oz) chestnut
   mushrooms, 300 g
   (10½ oz) quartered and
   the remainder diced

5 x 45 g (1½ oz) filo pastry
   sheets, measuring
   50 x 24 cm (20 x 9½ inches)

2 tablespoons chopped fresh
   chives

80 g (3 oz) Stilton cheese,
   crumbled

1 small onion, diced

2 tablespoons half fat crème
   fraîche

1½ teaspoons wholegrain
   mustard

1 tablespoon chopped fresh
   parsley

salt and freshly ground black
   pepper

This impressive vegetarian dish is a meal in itself. Serve with a fresh colourful salad.

1 Preheat the oven to Gas Mark 6/200°C/fan oven 180°C. Spray a lidded non stick saucepan with the cooking spray, add the leeks and quartered mushrooms, cover and leave them to sweat for 15 minutes, stirring occasionally. Remove the pan from the heat and leave to cool slightly.

2 Place one sheet of filo pastry on the work surface. Spray it with the cooking spray and then lay another sheet on top and spray again. Repeat this until all the sheets are used.

3 Add the chives, Stilton cheese and seasoning to the leek and mushroom mixture and mix well. Spoon the mixture down the centre of the stack of filo pastry sheets. Tuck the sides in and roll the pastry up, completely sealing the mixture in.

4 Place the strudel on a non stick baking tray with the join underneath and spray it with the cooking spray. Cook for 20 minutes or until golden.

5 Meanwhile, spray a small non stick saucepan with the cooking spray and add the onion and diced mushrooms. Stir fry for 5–6 minutes before adding the remaining ingredients. Check the seasoning.

6 When the strudel is cooked, remove from the oven and cut it into four slices. Serve each portion with a spoonful of sauce.

Variation... For a meaty version, see the recipe on page 81.

Soufflé baked potatoes

Serves 2

320 calories per serving

Takes 15 minutes to prepare,
  1 hour 15 minutes to cook

**2 x 300 g (10½ oz) baking
  potatoes**

**calorie controlled cooking
  spray**

**a small bunch of spring
  onions, sliced finely**

4 tablespoons skimmed milk

**50 g (1¾ oz) cherry
  tomatoes, quartered**

1 egg white

**50 g (1¾ oz) half fat Cheddar
  cheese, grated**

**salt and freshly ground black
  pepper**

*Simple baked potatoes take on an exciting new character
with a light cheese and onion filling. Serve these with a
crisp salad.*

1 Preheat the oven to Gas Mark 5/190°C/fan oven 170°C.
Prick the potatoes all over with a fork and bake for 1 hour
or until soft.

2 Meanwhile, heat a non stick frying pan, spray with the
cooking spray and stir fry the spring onions until just tender
and golden.

3 Cut the potatoes in half and scoop out the flesh into a large
bowl. Add the milk and mash together until you have a smooth
blend. Stir in the fried spring onions and the tomatoes and
season.

4 In a clean, grease-free bowl, whisk the egg white until stiff
and fluffy and then fold carefully into the potato mixture with
the grated cheese.

5 Place the potato skins on a non stick baking tray and refill
them with the potato mixture, piling it up high. Bake for
10–15 minutes, until golden and hot. Serve immediately.

Vegetarian moussaka

Serves 4

320 calories per serving

Takes 30 minutes to prepare,
45 minutes to cook

❄

**400 g (14 oz) potatoes,
peeled**

1 onion, chopped finely

2 garlic cloves, crushed

300 g (10½ oz) Quorn mince

**400 g can chopped tomatoes
with herbs**

**150 ml (5 fl oz) vegetable
stock**

2 tablespoons cornflour

1 large aubergine, sliced

1 egg

**125 g (4½ oz) low fat soft
cheese**

**150 g (5½ oz) 0% fat Greek
yogurt**

**25 g (1 oz) half fat mature
Cheddar cheese, grated**

**salt and freshly ground black
pepper**

*This is a vegetarian version of the traditional Moussaka on
page 86.*

1 Preheat the oven to Gas Mark 5/190°C/fan oven 170°C.
Bring a saucepan of water to the boil, add the potatoes and
cook for 8–10 minutes until just tender. Drain, allow to cool
and then slice thinly.

2 Dry fry the onion and garlic in a large non stick saucepan
for about 5–6 minutes, until browned.

3 Add the Quorn, tomatoes and stock, bring to the boil, then
reduce the heat and simmer for 10 minutes without a lid. Blend
the cornflour to a paste with 5 tablespoons of cold water, add
to the pan and stir until thickened. Season.

4 Spoon half the mince mixture into a large ovenproof baking
dish. Lay the aubergine slices on top. Spread the remaining
mince mixture over them and then arrange the sliced potatoes
on top in an overlapping layer.

5 Beat together the egg, soft cheese, yogurt and seasoning.
Spread this over the potatoes. Sprinkle with the cheese and
then bake for about 45 minutes, until the topping is set and
golden brown.

Quorn chicory bake

Serves 4

258 calories per serving

Takes 15 minutes to prepare, 45 minutes to cook

calorie controlled cooking spray

1 small red onion, chopped finely

200 g (7 oz) low fat soft cheese with garlic and herbs

50 ml (2 fl oz) vegetable stock

350 g packet Quorn Chicken Style Pieces

2 small chicory bulbs, sliced thickly

350 g (12 oz) Charlotte potatoes, peeled and cut into thin wedges lengthways

This is a lovely vegetarian version of the recipe on page 60.

1 Preheat the oven to Gas Mark 6/200°C/fan oven 180°C. Heat a large non stick frying pan and spray with the cooking spray. Add the onion and cook for 3 minutes until softened but not brown.

2 Remove from the heat and stir in the soft cheese and vegetable stock until smooth. Stir in the Quorn and chicory and spoon into a 1.2 litre (2 pint) ovenproof dish. Top with the potato wedges, spray with the cooking spray and bake in the oven for 45 minutes until golden and cooked. Serve immediately.

Tip... Chicory is also know as Belgian endive and is available in yellow or red varieties.

Cowboy pie

Serves 4

333 calories per serving

Takes 20 minutes to prepare,
25 minutes to cook

**calorie controlled cooking
spray**
1 onion, chopped
**200 ml (7 fl oz) vegetable
stock**
350 g packet Quorn mince
**420 g can low fat low salt
baked beans**
230 g can chopped tomatoes
**750 g (1 lb 10 oz) potatoes,
peeled and cut into 5 mm
(¼ inch) slices**
**salt and freshly ground black
pepper**

*This hearty dish is a delicious vegetarian take on a
shepherd's pie.*

1 Preheat the oven to Gas Mark 7/220°C/fan oven 200°C.
Heat a large non stick saucepan and spray with the cooking
spray. Add the onion and cook for 5 minutes until softened,
adding a splash of vegetable stock if it starts to stick.

2 Stir in the Quorn mince, beans, chopped tomatoes and
remaining stock, season, simmer for 5 minutes and then
pour into an ovenproof baking dish.

3 Bring a large saucepan of water to the boil and add the
sliced potatoes. Stir so that they don't stick together and cook
gently for 4 minutes or until tender but not falling apart.

4 Drain the potatoes carefully and arrange on top of the mince
mixture. Lightly spray with the cooking spray and bake in the
oven for 25 minutes until the topping is golden and crisp.

Winter mushrooms pot

Serves 2
199 calories per serving
Takes 10 minutes to prepare,
  30 minutes to cook

**calorie controlled cooking
  spray**
1 small leek, sliced finely
1 carrot, peeled and sliced
1 garlic clove, crushed
4 fresh thyme sprigs
250 g (9 oz) small chestnut
  mushrooms, halved
75 g (2¾ oz) whole cooked
  chestnuts, chopped roughly
2 teaspoons plain flour
50 ml (2 fl oz) marsala wine
400 ml (14 fl oz) vegetable
  stock
25 g (1 oz) dried mixed
  mushrooms
salt and freshly ground black
  pepper

Cooked chestnuts help to thicken this stew, but they also add a warming sweetness to the dish. Serve with 100 g (3½ oz) of boiled potatoes per person and cooked green beans.

1 Heat a large non stick saucepan and spray with the cooking spray. Add the leek and carrot and cook for 3–4 minutes. Spray the pan again and add the garlic, thyme, chestnut mushrooms and chestnuts. Cook for 2 minutes, stirring.

2 Sprinkle over the flour and then pour in the wine, stirring for 30 seconds. Gradually stir in the stock and then add the dried mushrooms and bring to the boil. Simmer gently for 30 minutes until thickened. Check the seasoning and serve immediately.

Spiced sweet potato tarte tatin

Serves 4

226 calories per serving

Takes 25 minutes to prepare,
30 minutes to cook

500 g (1 lb 2 oz) sweet
potatoes, peeled and sliced
thinly

calorie controlled cooking
spray

½ onion, sliced thinly

1 red chilli, de-seeded and
diced finely

2 tablespoons light brown
soft sugar

1 teaspoon baharat or Middle
Eastern spice blend

8 x 15 g (½ oz) filo pastry
sheets, measuring
30 x 40 cm (12 x 16 inches)

salt

1 tablespoon roughly
chopped fresh coriander
leaves, to garnish

*This easy tart is great served with a 30 g (1¼ oz) slice
of French stick, a wild rocket and tomato salad and
2 tablespoons of tzatziki per person.*

1 Preheat the oven to Gas Mark 4/180°C/fan oven 160°C. Put
the sweet potato slices in a large saucepan and cover with cold
water. Bring to the boil and simmer for 5 minutes.

2 Meanwhile, heat a non stick frying pan and spray with the
cooking spray. Add the onion and chilli and cook for 3 minutes
until starting to soften. Add the sugar, baharat or spice blend
and 3 tablespoons of cold water. Gently heat until the sugar has
dissolved, stirring occasionally. Bubble rapidly for 2 minutes
until reduced and syrupy. Season with a little salt.

3 Drain the potato slices and pat dry with kitchen towel. Add
to the frying pan and turn to coat in the onion syrup. Transfer
to a shallow 20 cm (8 inch) round cake tin or tarte tatin dish,
levelling the top.

4 Spray each sheet of filo pastry with the cooking spray and
lay on the top of the potato, pushing the pastry down the sides
of the tin and arranging it so that it completely covers the top
of the potatoes.

5 Bake in the oven for 30 minutes until golden. Leave to cool
in the tin for 5 minutes before upturning on to a plate. Scatter
over the coriander, cut into wedges and serve immediately.

Tip... If you have an ovenproof frying pan, leave the sweet
potato mixture in the pan at the end of step 2. Top with the
pastry as in step 3, then bake as above.

Desserts and bakes

Orange and lemon cheesecake

A bright citrus cheesecake to lighten the depths of winter.

Serves 8

224 calories per serving

Takes 25 minutes + 3 hours chilling

❄ (undecorated)

50 g (1¾ oz) low fat spread

2 teaspoons golden syrup

150 g (5½ oz) light digestive biscuits, crushed

2 oranges, peeled and segmented, to decorate

For the topping

200 g (7 oz) low fat soft cheese

50 g (1¾ oz) fructose

grated zest and juice of a lemon

grated zest and juice of an orange

11 g sachet gelatine

300 g (10½ oz) low fat orange or lemon flavoured yogurt

1 egg white

1 Melt the low fat spread and golden syrup together in a pan and thoroughly mix in the biscuit crumbs. Press this mixture firmly into the base of a 20 cm (8 inch) loose bottomed springform tin. Chill while you prepare the topping.

2 Beat together the soft cheese, fructose, lemon zest, lemon juice and orange zest.

3 Place the orange juice in a small heatproof bowl, sprinkle the gelatine over it and leave to stand for 5 minutes, until it becomes spongy. Place the bowl over a pan of gently simmering water and heat until clear and the gelatine has completely dissolved. Allow to cool for 5 minutes.

4 Beat the gelatine into the soft cheese mixture with the yogurt. In a clean, grease-free bowl, whisk the egg white until it forms soft peaks. Fold into the cheese and yogurt mixture.

5 Spoon the topping over the biscuit base, level the top and leave to chill for at least 3 hours.

6 To serve, carefully remove from the tin on to a serving plate and arrange the orange segments around the edge.

Citrus chocolate spice pudding

Serves 4
175 calories per serving
Takes 20 minutes

calorie controlled cooking
  spray
**100 g (3½ oz) grapefruit
  segments**
**½ teaspoon ground ginger
  (optional)**
**4 heaped teaspoons reduced
  sugar marmalade**
50 g (1¾ oz) caster sugar
2 eggs
50 g (1¾ oz) self raising flour
15 g (½ oz) cocoa powder

*If you've never cooked a sponge like this, you're in for a
treat, as it literally rises in front of your eyes.*

1 Spray a 1.2 litre (2 pint) pudding basin with the cooking spray
and put the grapefruit segments into the basin. Mix the ginger, if
using, and 2 teaspoons of water into the marmalade and spoon
this mixture over the grapefruit.

2 Using an electric beater, whisk the sugar and eggs together
until very light and thick; this will take about 5 minutes.

3 Sift the flour and cocoa powder together and then gently fold
into the whisked mixture, using a large metal spoon to retain as
much air as possible. Transfer this mixture to the pudding basin.

4 To cook in the microwave, cover the basin with microwave
safe cling film and pierce it two or three times. Cook in the
microwave on high for 2½–3 minutes, or until risen and spongy.
Allow to stand for 3 minutes before serving.

Tip... To cook in a steamer, cover the pudding with foil or
greaseproof paper and steam for 1 hour 10 minutes, making
sure that the steamer does not boil dry.

Variation... Use a peeled and segmented orange – with all
the pith removed – instead of the grapefruit segments.

Christmas ice cream

Serves 8

112 calories per serving

Takes 10 minutes + 6 hours to freeze + 30 minutes resting

○ (if using vegetarian mincemeat)

❄

150 g (5½ oz) mincemeat

8 g sachet dried egg white powder

450 g (1 lb) low fat vanilla yogurt

50 g (1¾ oz) light digestive biscuits, chopped roughly

grated zest of ½ an orange

200 g (7 oz) low fat custard

2 teaspoons ground cinnamon

This frozen dessert tastes like crushed mince pies and cream. For a real taste of Christmas, serve 100 g (3½ oz) in bowls with half a drained 210 g can of cocktail fruit in natural juice per person.

1 Put the mincemeat in a small pan and gently heat until the suet has melted. Set aside. In a bowl, dissolve the egg white powder according to the packet instructions. Using an electric hand whisk, whisk until stiff peaks are formed. In another bowl, mix together the yogurt, biscuits, orange zest, custard, cinnamon and mincemeat.

2 Using a large metal spoon, carefully fold the egg white into the custard mixture and then spoon the mixture into a shallow freezerproof container. Put in the freezer for 2 hours.

3 After 2 hours, the ice cream should have started to freeze around the edges. Using a fork, whip the frozen mixture, breaking up the ice crystals. Return to the freezer for another 2 hours. Repeat once more and freeze for at least another 2 hours or until needed.

4 To serve, remove from the freezer 30 minutes before eating.

Tip... Dried egg white is pasteurised and available in most large supermarkets. It is in the baking section of the supermarket, near the gelatine.

Baby bread and butter puds

Serves 4

298 calories per serving

Takes 25 minutes to prepare
 + 30 minutes standing,
 20–30 minutes to cook

1 tablespoon mixed peel
 (optional)

50 g (1¾ oz) sultanas or
 raisins

grated zest of a lemon or
 small orange

6 medium slices white bread,
 crusts removed

4 teaspoons low fat spread

calorie controlled cooking
 spray

350 ml (12 fl oz) skimmed
 milk

3 tablespoons soft brown
 sugar

2 eggs

These delightful individual puddings are great for portion control.

1 Mix the peel, if using, with the sultanas or raisins and lemon or orange zest.

2 Using pastry cutters, cut 12 discs out of the bread to fit inside four medium ramekins. Spread the bread discs lightly with the low fat spread.

3 Spray the insides of the ramekins with the cooking spray and then place a bread disc in the bottom of each one. Divide half the fruit mixture evenly between the ramekins. Repeat the layer of bread and fruit and top with a bread disc; the low fat spread side should face up.

4 In a small non stick saucepan, bring the milk to the boil with the sugar, stirring until the sugar has dissolved. Remove the pan from the heat and set aside to cool for 5 minutes.

5 Beat the eggs in a large heatproof bowl, add the milk mixture to the eggs and beat well. Slowly pour the mixture over each filled ramekin, making sure it seeps inside.

6 Leave the ramekins for about 30 minutes to allow the bread to absorb the liquid. Preheat the oven to Gas Mark 5/190°C/fan oven 170°C.

7 Stand the ramekins in a small roasting tin and pour hot water into the tin so that it comes two thirds of the way up the dishes. Bake for 20–30 minutes or until risen, golden and crisp on top. Remove the ramekins from the tin and allow them to stand for 5 minutes before serving.

Crêpes suzette

Serves 4
158 calories per serving
Takes 20 minutes

50 g (1¾ oz) plain flour
a pinch of salt
1 egg
125 ml (4 fl oz) skimmed milk
calorie controlled cooking spray
312 g can mandarin orange segments in natural juice, drained and juice reserved
2 tablespoons reduced sugar orange marmalade
1 orange, peeled and segmented

To serve
4 tablespoons low fat natural yogurt
a few fresh mint sprigs

Pancakes are not just for Pancake Day. This is a lovely zingy dessert to chase away the winter blues.

1 In a bowl, whisk together the flour, salt and egg. Gradually whisk in the milk until the batter is smooth.

2 Heat a non stick frying pan and spray with the cooking spray. Spoon a ladleful of batter into the pan and swirl around to spread the mixture. Cook for 1–2 minutes, turning over halfway, until golden. Transfer to a plate. Repeat with the batter to make three more pancakes, spraying the frying pan with the cooking spray each time. Fold the pancakes into quarters and set aside.

3 Put the mandarin juice and marmalade into the frying pan and gently heat. Add the orange and mandarin segments and pancakes. Gently heat for 1–2 minutes until the pancakes have heated through and the juice has thickened. Serve with the yogurt and garnished with the mint sprigs.

Jam roly poly

Serves 6
201 calories per serving
Takes 25 minutes to prepare,
  1½ hours to cook

calorie controlled cooking
  spray
200 g (7 oz) self raising flour
½ teaspoon salt
100 g (3½ oz) low fat spread
**6 tablespoons reduced sugar
  strawberry or raspberry
  jam**
**a little skimmed milk, for
  brushing**

*This recipe will take you back to your childhood. It's a
proper stodgy, steamed version but made with low fat
spread rather than suet. The result is well worth the wait.*

1 Half fill a steamer with water and put on to boil (see Tip).
Spray a piece of foil measuring 23 x 33 cm (9 x 13 inches)
with the cooking spray.

2 In a large bowl, mix together the flour, salt and low fat spread.
Add about 7 tablespoons of water, mix to form a light elastic
dough and then knead this very lightly until smooth. Roll out on
a floured surface to a 23 x 25 cm (9 x 11 inches) oblong.

3 Spread the pastry with the jam, leaving a 5 mm (¼ inch) clear
border all round. Brush the edges with a little skimmed milk and
roll the pastry up evenly, starting from one of the short sides.

4 Place the roll on the foil and wrap the foil loosely around, to
allow for expansion, but seal the edges very well. Place the roll
in the steamer and cover. Steam over rapidly boiling water for
1½ hours. Remove from the foil and serve.

Tip... If you do not have a steamer, you can use a large pan
with a close fitting lid. You could also cover the pan with
foil or baking parchment and then put on the lid so that it is
sealed even better. Be sure to keep an eye on the water level
and top it up with boiling water if necessary.

Sticky toffee pudding

Serves 6
321 calories per serving
Takes 10 minutes to prepare,
   45 minutes to cook

There is no need to miss out on scrumptious treats, as this recipe proves.

1 Preheat the oven to Gas Mark 5/190°C/fan oven 170°C. Spray a 19 cm (7½ inch) square cake tin with the cooking spray and line the base with non stick baking parchment.

2 Place the dates in a small pan with 200 ml (7 fl oz) of water. Bring to the boil and simmer for 5 minutes, by which time the dates will have absorbed most of the water. Stir in the bicarbonate of soda.

calorie controlled cooking spray
175 g (6 oz) stoned dates, chopped
1 teaspoon bicarbonate of soda
175 g (6 oz) self raising flour
175 g (6 oz) dark muscovado sugar
50 g (1¾ oz) low fat spread
3 tablespoons skimmed milk
1 teaspoon vanilla essence
2 egg whites

For the sticky sauce
1 tablespoon dark muscovado sugar
1 tablespoon golden syrup
4 tablespoons virtually fat free fromage frais

3 Place the flour, sugar and low fat spread in a bowl and rub together until the fat has been incorporated into the flour and the mixture is crumbly. Stir in the milk, vanilla essence and dates.

4 In a clean, grease-free bowl, whisk the egg whites until they form soft peaks. Fold into the pudding mixture and then spoon the mixture into the cake tin. Level the surface and bake for 35 minutes or until well risen and firm.

5 To make the sauce, place all the ingredients in a small pan and heat until melted and smooth. Do not allow the mixture to boil.

6 Serve the pudding warm, with a drizzle of the sauce.

Tip... This pudding is also delicious eaten cold, so save a slice for a day later, to enjoy with a cup of coffee. You can also serve the pudding as a teatime cake.

Rhubarb and ginger crumble

Serves 6

255 calories per serving

Takes 20 minutes to prepare,
20–30 minutes to cook

Everyone seems to love this pudding – it is a perfect combination of sweet and tart, juicy and crunchy and very quick and easy to make.

1 Preheat the oven to Gas Mark 6/200°C/fan oven 180°C. Place all the fruit ingredients in a 1 litre (1¾ pint) ovenproof dish.

2 In a bowl, make the crumble by rubbing the low fat spread into both flours until the mixture is the texture of fine breadcrumbs. Stir in the other ingredients.

3 Sprinkle the crumble on top of the fruit and bake for 20–30 minutes or until the fruit is bubbling up the sides of the dish and the topping is golden and crunchy

Tip... You can use fresh rhubarb instead of canned fruit; just increase the cooking time to 30–40 minutes so the fruit becomes soft and juicy.

For the fruit

2 x 400 g cans rhubarb in light syrup

2 teaspoons rose water (optional)

2 tablespoons clear honey

For the crumble

75 g (2¾ oz) low fat spread

100 g (3½ oz) plain flour

100 g (3½ oz) wholemeal flour

50 g (1¾ oz) golden granulated sugar

50 g (1¾ oz) stem ginger, chopped

1 teaspoon ground ginger

Christmas filo tartlets

Serves 8

90 calories per serving

Takes 15 minutes to prepare,
20–25 minutes to cook +
cooling

⚥ (if using vegetarian
mincemeat)

4 x 15 g (½ oz) filo pastry
sheets, measuring
30 x 40 cm (12 x 16 inches),
each cut into six squares

15 g (½ oz) low fat spread,
melted

150 g (5½ oz) mincemeat

1 large eating apple, peeled
and cored

1 teaspoon icing sugar, for
dusting

*Grated apple is added to the mincemeat, making it lighter
and less rich.*

1 Preheat the oven to Gas Mark 5/190°C/fan oven 170°C. Brush
a square of filo pastry with the melted low fat spread and place
in the base of one hole of a 12 hole non stick bun tin. Layer with
another two squares at angles and then repeat to make eight
tartlet cases.

2 Place the mincemeat in a bowl, grate in the apple and mix
well. Place a spoonful of mixture into each case and gently press
down the pastry corners, leaving the middle exposed. Bake for
20–25 minutes until the pastry is golden. Cool in the tin before
dusting with the icing sugar. Serve warm.

Tip... These store in an airtight container for up to 2 days.

Rich dark fruit cake

Makes 20 slices
270 calories per slice
Takes 25 minutes to prepare, 1¾ hours to cook
Ⓥ
❄

350 g (12 oz) ready to eat prunes	1 cooking apple, peeled, cored and grated
6 tablespoons brandy or sherry	350 g (12 oz) plain flour
finely grated zest and juice of a large lemon	2 teaspoons baking powder
finely grated zest and juice of a large orange	2 teaspoons mixed spice
200 g (7 oz) dark muscovado sugar	½ teaspoon ground nutmeg
4 eggs	800 g (1 lb 11 oz) luxury dried mixed fruit
1 tablespoon black treacle	6 tablespoons semi skimmed milk

We all have a favourite rich fruit cake recipe. But at times when we want to have that special celebration cake without the high fat content, isn't it great to have an alternative recipe that means you can stick to tradition without it sticking to the hips.

1 Heat the oven to Gas Mark 4/180°C/fan oven 160°C. Line a deep 23 cm (9 inch) round cake tin with non stick baking parchment.

2 Purée the prunes in a food processor or liquidiser, together with the brandy or sherry and lemon and orange zest and juice. Transfer to a bowl and whisk in the sugar and eggs until the mixture becomes light and fluffy. Whisk in the treacle.

3 Use a metal spoon to stir in the apple, flour, baking powder and spices. Finally mix in the dried fruit and enough milk to form a soft dropping consistency. Transfer to the prepared tin, levelling out the surface.

continues overleaf ▶

▶ Rich dark fruit cake *continued*

4 Bake in the centre of the oven for 45 minutes. Reduce the oven temperature to Gas Mark 3/ 160°C/fan oven 140°C and continue to cook for 1 hour or until the cake is well risen and a skewer inserted in the centre comes out clean.

5 Leave the cake to cool in the tin before removing and discarding the baking parchment. Wrap the cake in fresh paper or foil and store in an airtight tin. The cake is best left for at least a day to mature before cutting.

Tip... An old wives' tale or not, try leaving a whole apple in the storage container alongside fruit cakes to help keep them moist.

Variation... To decorate the cake, brush the surface with 1 tablespoon of apricot jam and roll out 175 g (6 oz) of ready to roll icing. Press firmly on to the cake, trim the edges and decorate with strips of lemon or orange rind.

Hot trifle

Serves 4
111 calories per serving
Takes 20 minutes to prepare,
10 minutes to bake

4 sponge fingers
**275 g (9½ oz) frozen
raspberries, defrosted**
**100 ml (3½ fl oz) cranberry
juice**
**1 tablespoon artificial
sweetener**
150 g (5½ oz) low fat custard
2 egg whites
25 g (1 oz) caster sugar

*Trifle is such a versatile dessert as you can use so many
different combinations of fruit. This hot version is a
wonderful treat for a special meal.*

1 Preheat the oven to Gas Mark 5/190°C/fan oven 170°C.
Break each sponge finger into pieces and divide them between
four heatproof dishes – glass ramekins are ideal as then you
can see all the layers.

2 Mix together the raspberries, cranberry juice and sweetener
and spoon this on top of the sponge pieces. Spoon equal
amounts of custard over each dish.

3 In a clean, grease-free bowl, whisk the egg whites until they
form soft peaks. Fold in the sugar and then whisk again until
you have a glossy meringue mixture.

4 Spoon the meringue mixture over each dish and use the
back of a spoon to form rough peaks. Bake for 10 minutes,
until the meringue topping is pale golden. Serve at once.

Variation... Other fruits, such as sliced strawberries or
blueberries, can be used instead of raspberries.

Cranberry spiced muffins

Makes 12 muffins
179 calories per serving
Takes 15 minutes to prepare,
20 minutes to bake

300 g (10½ oz) plain flour
2 teaspoons baking powder
½ teaspoon ground
   cinnamon
½ teaspoon ground nutmeg
finely grated zest of an
   orange
125 g (4½ oz) demerara
   sugar
75 g (2¾ oz) frozen
   cranberries, defrosted
50 ml (2 fl oz) sunflower oil
225 ml (8 fl oz) skimmed
   milk
1 egg

These days, cranberries are easily available all year round.
They add a wonderful tang to these delicious muffins.

1 Preheat the oven to Gas Mark 6/200°C/fan oven 180°C.
Line a 12 hole muffin tray with paper cases.

2 Sift the flour and baking powder into a mixing bowl and stir
in the cinnamon, nutmeg and orange zest. Add the sugar and
cranberries.

3 Beat together the oil, milk and egg and pour this over the
dry ingredients. Mix well with a wooden spoon to make a soft
batter. Spoon the mixture into the paper cases and bake for
15–20 minutes, until the muffins are well risen and golden.

Variation... Cranberries are quite a sharp fruit – if you
prefer something sweeter, use sultanas or raisins instead.

Walnut brownies

Makes 16 slices

103 calories per serving

Takes 15 minutes to prepare,
  25 minutes to bake +
  cooling

175 g (6 oz) self raising flour,
  sifted

a pinch of salt

2 tablespoons drinking
  chocolate

50 g (1¾ oz) light brown soft
  sugar

100 g (3½ oz) low fat spread,
  melted

1 tablespoon white wine
  vinegar

1 teaspoon vanilla essence

50 g (1¾ oz) walnuts,
  chopped

A delicious treat with a cup of coffee on a cold winter's day.

1 Preheat the oven to Gas Mark 4/180°C/fan oven 160°C. Line a 20 cm (8 inch) square tin with non stick baking parchment.

2 Place the flour, salt, drinking chocolate and sugar in a large bowl and stir to combine. Add the low fat spread, vinegar, vanilla essence, walnuts and 200 ml (7 fl oz) of cold water. Beat well to make sure there are no lumps of flour left.

3 Tip into the baking tin and bake for 25 minutes. Leave to cool in the tin for 15 minutes before slicing into 16 squares. Transfer to a wire rack and allow to cool completely before eating.

Index